Becoming...
Mr. Henry

One Man's Path From Learning to Teaching

by Peter Henry

CYNTOMedia
CORPORATION

Pittsburgh, PA

ISBN 1-58501-087-1

Trade Paperback
© Copyright 2005 Peter Henry
All Rights Reserved
First Printing — 2005
Library of Congress #2004117542

Request for information should be addressed to:

SterlingHouse Publisher, Inc.
7436 Washington Avenue
Pittsburgh, PA 15218
www.sterlinghousepublisher.com

SterlingHouse Publisher, Inc. is a company
of the CyntoMedia Corporation.

Cover Design: Jonah Lloyd
Cover Art: Jonah Lloyd
Typesetting & Layout Design: Beth Buckholtz

Printed in the United States of America

table of contents

I. What's In A Name? 1

Part I: Teacher Training

II. Professors Of The Baby Boom 10
III. Picture A Thousand Stories 15
IV. No Child's Story Left Behind 21
V. The Odd Couple 35
VI. Into The Looking Glass 41
VII. You Want To Be A Teacher? 59

Part II: Teacher in Residence

VIII. Aissatou Angel 80
IX. A Dozen Things About Teaching For Five Minutes 87
X. Bad Days And Sleepless Nights 109
XI. Play 115
XII. No Sex, No Drugs, No Rock N' Roll 133
XIII. Brown vs. The Board 157
XIV. Post-Script And Mortems 177

acknowledgement

Dedicated with love to my parents, Betty and Ed, who were dedicated to us and to all children and students who needed to find their voice or someone to believe in. What you gave to me has been priceless and I love you very much. And also, thanks to my beautiful wife, Lisa, whose hard work, steadfast support and deep love helped make this possible.

Thanks also to teachers everywhere, and mine in particular in St. Cloud, South Bend, Burlington, Northfield and Minneapolis who make appearances in this book, as well as others too numerous to mention. There is no greater profession. Thanks to friends who took time from their busy lives to read and critique this manuscript: Charlie, Anne, Michelle, Spruce, Celia, Marcobia, John, Bruce, Maralee and Tamson. Your help and support was greatly appreciated.

Thanks to the guys at Rising Sun for providing me with a happy place to land on Wednesday nights far from the madding crowd. Thanks to Evelyn and Arnie Olson for believing in me at a crucial time, making my dream come true at Wagon Landing. Thanks to my brothers and sisters for assistance large and small when I was young and fearful. It was a great life growing up together.

Some names in this book have been changed to protect people's privacy. A few teachers depicted here are composites of actual individuals I have known but otherwise all the material, people and events that I describe in this book are true to my memory.

what's in a name?

Here is a subtle but radical concept: We are all students; we are all teachers. Subtle because it rolls so easily off the tongue it is tempting to overlook or ignore. Radical because if we really understand what it means and embrace it, everything changes in education and our society. That as much as it takes a village to raise a child, it takes children to raise — and certainly to make — a village.

We are all students; we are all teachers.

How do I know? Because I have watched my little god-child at three years old kissing and caring for his younger brother not yet one, introducing him to the world, to their family. Because I have seen my mother at age 80 — a teacher herself — learn to walk again, to eat again, to start life over after a serious stroke paralyzed the left side of her body. Because every day, young people not yet competent by virtue of a high school diploma are left to babysit children, to teach them about sharing and basic realities of right and wrong. Because I have experienced it myself, growing from a small handful of piss and vinegar into one trusted to lead young people into discovery and a surer facility with their skills. Because I have witnessed over the course of this journey how much there is to learn about being a teacher, about kids and adults, about our common humanity.

We are all students; we are all teachers. The only questions are how much we enjoy each role and whether we pursue them with passion, curiosity and love.

I understand that it may sound trite, even beyond the point of our current predicament. America likes to draw rigid lines, proclaim who is the learner and teacher, then demand results. We make it clear — *You are a student:* do this, do that, and mostly, this is what you can't do. And for the other — *You are a teacher:* do this, do that, and mostly, this is what you must do. It makes for order, efficiency and a compliant citizenry, thus I don't expect it to change soon. In fact, it seems all we can manage in education at this point is to fend off a massive backwards lurch into re-segregated schools, federal testing requirements, a standardized curriculum and unseemly efforts to punish anyone and everyone standing in the way.

For me, it seems like a remarkable admission of failure — after thousands of years of organized learning — to not quite understand or value the educational process for every person, but simply throw stock requirements at them. For others, I realize, it is particularly upsetting that we cannot get everyone to read or write at the same level, and especially to pass basic tests in math, geography or history. But our collective disappointment, emerging from opposite ends of the education spectrum, is beside the point. Such are the demands of teaching that we must start over every day, every moment and build from where we are — not lament what has gone wrong or get dispirited about circumstances. We are where we are. Calling it a crisis, a national scandal or even just a damn shame will not change anything, especially for young people who hope more than anyone for a decent future.

We can and should debate what hurts, what helps and how the system can improve, but ultimately, the best thing for us to do is acknowledge our standing as both student and teacher and be inspired in our roles. That as sure as we may be about something, its truth and importance, we must sit down and listen, open our curiosity to more perspectives and data and see if it is calling us to a larger understanding — or a larger responsibility to help others understand. That in acknowledging that each of us is valuable and vulnerable — must at times teach as well as learn — we will shift the focus of education away from scape-goating, crisis and culture wars to something deeper, more personal, and ultimately, much more fulfilling.

* * *

When I was a novice teacher, the very first student who entered my classroom on the first night of orientation was a pert young woman with closely cropped hair and a nose stud. I felt excited, thrilled about my new profession. "What's your name?" I bubbled out.

"Sunshine," she said evenly, "Sunshine Miller." *What a great name*, I thought to myself, how wholly appropriate to start my adventure with a student named Sunshine. I was huddled in an ancient, high-ceilinged room with wood floors, archaic desks, traditional blackboards and great single-paned windows overlooking a statue of Jean-Baptiste De La Salle, the patron saint of Catholic education. It was a very antiquated place to begin, and in truth, I had no idea what I was doing.

"And you are...?"

I hesitated just a little. "I am...Pete...Mr. Henry." It had been a good 10 months since I was a student teacher and it still felt awkward. At age 27, in all honesty, I began without ever having been called Mr. Henry or even having thought of myself as anything other than a happy-go-lucky kid who'd graduated from college a few years back. Not to mention the ambivalence I felt about my role as teacher in a Catholic school which radiated tradition, formality, even intimidation. "Nice to meet you, Sunshine." I managed.

That was a start, not just as a teacher but also as a student of teaching, of learning the importance of every little thing, the most basic of which began right then — using names — an aptitude for which I demonstrated instant facility. I took to it, and however chaotic or unfocused my lessons, I hung on doggedly to student's names each and every day, each and every time I called on them. It's tricky to explain why it matters; I only know that it does. That it rewards every youngster for being unique — a person recognized, valuable and important enough to have their name called out-loud in the public square. And to do it as much as possible in a positive sense, so that they and everyone, come to understand it as an affirmation of that person's identity, gifts and potential.

To this day I am struck dumb by the bunches of teachers I have known who had not yet mastered student's names by the time of fall parent conferences. How they would scramble to their grade book for the correct class and period, and then be able to give only a vague run-down of assignments turned in, attendance and the state of quiz scores. Wasn't it obvious the teacher hadn't the slightest idea or facility for that child's identity? Had no real idea what he or she even looked like? It must be the supreme irony of American education that we are completely willing to fail children for not knowing certain names and core material while simultaneously we would be unable to introduce them were they to land on our doorstep. We fail them for not learning what we want. But we also fail them, in a completely different sense, by not learning who they are. And what students learn in the process — that ignorance is tolerated, respect is optional, only conformity matters — damages them for life.

I prided myself on mastering every student's name, tuning in on some oddball habit, allowing each personality to shine in my mind. And at conferences, hardly a parent wanted a run-down of their child's grade column as much as to compare notes about their kid's quirks, character and aptitudes. They wanted feedback, new data on the pet project they were engaged with — not standard lines — and I felt happy to oblige.

Yet, as natural as I took to using names, it felt correspondingly unnatural to have *my* horn honked by a student I was just getting to know. Hearing my own name, crisp and decisive, was not something I had grown up with. Both of my parents floundered through a list of possibilities, "Steven, Michael, John" — all related to me — before finding Peter. For most of my life growing up, the importance of my family name preceded me, interpreted me, determined me — the end of a long line well known for...well, all kinds of things. Later, as an adolescent in a new and faraway town, I decided to keep it well hidden, as if stepping too far into the world of being named would stop me from becoming who I was really meant to be. I ducked more than embraced what my name said about me.

As a young teacher, I stumbled through with foils and masks. In French class, I was *Monsieur Henri*, in Spanish, *Señor Henry* — in both cases the "H" appropriately aspirated for linguistic accuracy — a foreign tongue between me and an identity. More troubling were occasional nicknames, jabs, attempts to rattle my cage by way of finding a suitable moniker for an instructor not yet house broken: "Hey Peter," "Pee-Pee," "Hen-House," "Hen-Dog" and other fun things leaked out during class, the attendant twittering and snickers designed to injure as much as express glee. "Woodstock" (the concert, not the bird) seemed to catch on at one point, a couple of suburban stoners confident they had captured something ineffable, though what, besides my '70s wardrobe and the fact I rode bike to school, was never clear. I went by "Coach" with players, got it shortened to "Henry" by others and was content to go through the week unaware and unconcerned about what I was called or whether it mattered.

Only now does the whole thing feels even remotely notable. At some point, "Mr. Henry" lodged in people's minds. Again, it didn't matter to me, but for others it acquired a level of suitability and precision which made a fit. Despite an openness to being called "Peter" if students felt they knew me, none did; and colleagues at school, parents and administrators inclined toward "Mr. Henry" well after we made it to a first-name basis. Even my friends and wife have taken it up on occasion as a substantial statement about who I am. Like the heroic couplet in Tennyson's *Ulysses*, my personal trials and tribulations have become a name — despite my own obliviousness.

* * *

In *Genesis*, God assigns to man dominion over every animal that creepeth on land, or fowl that flyeth, or fish that swimeth at sea. The lynch pin of that dominion is that man gets to name these animals, and presumably, since they and nature are separate and distinct from humankind, use them as he — and eventually she — sees fit. That fundamental teaching has not been lost on us as we proceed through the bounty and spoils of nature. If we can name it, we can help ourselves to use, eat or extract it, at least in the Judeo-Christian world. There is too, even in traditional societies, the belief in the power of naming. That in many cultures, names — even for plants and animals — are earned on the basis of notable qualities or achievement; and also, that employing them accrues power for the user almost like a charm or incantation.

Far be it from me to suggest a reversal of such ancient practices, attitudes or hierarchies. I have come to my name wholly by virtue of having mastered so many. I look down from my perch and understand that the employment and gradual accretion of names over time has allowed me the position I hold: assimilated to my foundation is this mysterious power of calling out, and sometimes creating, identity in those around me. I see it but do not wholly understand it, which makes me more a student than anything. I only know how important it is, how crucial that we learn and use names — of all people — that we respect their character and be alert to this power, whether for Adam and Eve or more descriptive terms like "truant" or "failure" or "minority." Names pile around us as the reality of how we see the world and create the ground we walk upon.

That's why I insist that if we really understood the power of each of us being a student and a teacher, our society, and especially education, would change radically. I do not literally mean that children should take up teaching posts or that educators need more courses in psychology. Only that the realization that we still have much to learn — and a ton to learn about teaching — would benefit us greatly, and that to really understand that we need acknowledge being students ourselves. It would mean not seeing young people as blank slates to be trained in our image or according to standard formulas but as novice educators providing vital feedback and inspiration as to what is really important. And it would certainly mean learning their names and valuing their stories before asking them to memorize the ones so far removed. It would also mean not blaming their schools or teachers for shortcomings but assuming responsibility ourselves to make our children and the world better. Occasionally, it might mean rolling up our sleeves, walking to the corner and seeing what we can do to help, or at least to help ourselves understand what truths pervade there. To help us get to that more accessible place — to soften the tough muscle of the heart — we too, need hear our name called out loud in public and remember feeling powerless, vulnerable, not knowing yet wanting genuine answers. To be told to our face: "We are all students, and this means you (your name here)."

Which leads us to the somewhat awkward title (at least for me) of this book. I toyed with other names — *Schooled in America, The*

Education of a Teacher — and even submitted them feeling I had it pretty much nailed down. A part of me shudders at the perceived vanity or self-promotion involved in using my name in the title — *my own name for God sakes*! But this book was not written for me, nor because I have attained some privileged position in terms of teaching. It was written out of concern for how we convey young people to adulthood, to show that how it gets done is absolutely essential for that child — for all of us — and how teachers have a rare opportunity to influence and inspire that process. Over years I have been greatly touched to realize that "students" and "teachers" — whatever we call them or require of them — are first and foremost human beings, good and imperfect, and we need cherish the enduring paradox of what that means.

In the end, I do believe there is power in using my real name. That it validates the process I have been using, as well as the thousands of students who once experienced its effect or believed in it — that they more than anyone nominated its title. In husk and fiber it manifests something tangible, and I need come forward now to claim it. I also consider that my identity as a teacher is not yet closed or complete, so "becoming" not only feels apt but leaves room for new experiences and hypotheses.

I am convinced that America's public needs to reacquaint itself with what happens in school, to take in stories from people who work there so as not to be easily fooled into notions of a "crisis" in education. If critics want to find a crisis, they should focus on the larger culture that accepts an unconscionable divide between rich and poor, festering racial inequities, a general breakdown of families and a reluctance to fund compensating public services out of a disdain for taxes. It is our mad rush to get ahead, to finish first in the race for social and material primacy which is creating the real crisis in America, engendering as it does legions of winners and losers and the general fear there will never be enough. Learning at school is too complicated, profound, even ancient to imagine that it has suddenly gone broke and must be repaired by adhering to national standards and a regime of "accountability" by exam, which is, after all, the ultimate platform for creating winners and losers. We might understand this if we listened closely to those working at school.

I have sifted through my past, followed yarns out the door, around corners, up or down into attic and basement, hoping to locate places where an active child once made small discoveries — listening, sharing, playing, imagining. It is not unusual to unpack a personal history, but it is a kind of departure from the standard approach of surfacing educational issues.

More typically, education authors stand apart from their identity as young people, convey the impression they are no longer students — haven't a whisper of childishness about them; but rather, are sturdy professionals with absolute authority over the material they represent.

I am taking a different tack and want to believe in its singular importance: again, not for myself, but for that ancient profession whose job it is to assist students find routes from unexplored attics, difficult basements into daylight and a kind of fellowship with the world. How we do this, that it gets done well makes a huge difference — for them, for all of us — so I believe each is worth conveying: my own route as a youngster, theirs, the way of teaching, that tracing each arc carefully to points of common intersection exposes something essential about education, about the connection in each our lives to being both a learner and a teacher, sometimes in the same breath. That's my intention in setting out, and I know this much for certain: intention — mission really — is always the heart of finding your way.

Part I:
Teacher Training

professors of the baby boom

Parents are our first teachers, the best and most profound introduction to the world we inhabit. Their care and sense of decency (or lack thereof) forever inform our living. Yet, as ideal as we like to imagine the world of a child, the reality of bringing one to life does not always go smooth. Not every pregnancy is greeted with jubilation, part of a comfortably planned life — nor are they even necessarily brought to term. And single and divorced parents now outnumber the old-fashioned nuclear family. Such is our modern condition that Freud believed young boys secretly wish to kill their father, marry their mother; Jung, that we must overcome issues which parents grapple with but don't fully resolve. The best of nesting pairs simply roll the dice and turn out young into a world of conflict, challenge and cross-tides — breakthroughs, triumph and moments of great joy and love. What combination of these we end up with becomes us and cannot be easily washed off or forgotten. Even the orphan Dorothy, getting a world-class education in far-away Oz desired only a single thing: to get back to Kansas and the psychic equivalent of mom and dad.

The most straight-forward claim I can make about my parents is that they were both teachers, the chalkboard kind, and that they were not satisfied with a small class but kept at it until they had one side of a baseball game, coaches at first and third. My mother was the eldest of eight in a North Dakota family that grew up largely without electricity or plumbing. Her mother, of a large Irish family, had been a rural school marm before marrying; her father, the youngest of eight in a frontier Norwegian household. My father came from a comparatively self-disciplined, well-to-do family of five, in the small regional center of St. Cloud. Together, his mother and father grew up on the frontier in families of 13 and 10 children, respectively. However demanding it may be today to bring children into the world, America's previous generations sure made short work of it.

My parent's story is not unlike millions of others in this country: small town upbringing, off to college, a blind date, World War II, correspondence, the Allied victory, and marriage followed by a string of new arrivals. The historical fact of the Baby Boom has dominated our family in a visceral, lasting and largely unspoken way — a constant toss of youngsters, more and always more children to plot with, to play and plan and pick teams. So saturated with young bodies was my life that, at times, I imagined there were no parents: that I floated on a cushion of kids, acting, talking, learning exactly like others but with little direct contact with the lords themselves.

I understand this cannot be entirely true. Someone runs the house, prepares meals, changes diapers, gives baths and gets children dressed for the world. My mother was particularly well-suited for it growing up during the Depression: learning thrift, economy and house-holding on the Dakota prairie. With a degree in English from a small Catholic college, she was also well positioned for being a teacher — and was one for several years before marrying. I imagine it was she who tied my shoes the first day I went to school; that she did it in that rhyming, talkative, cheerful way of hers: "All righty, Peter, Peter Pumpkin Eater, let's get those shoes tied tighty-tight-tight-tied." She enjoyed reading us *Mother Goose* at night, or *Christopher Robin*, or *Robin Hood*, and as much as she filled stomachs with homemade bread and bean soup at midday, we drifted off at night listening to her voice, tigers chasing, imagining far-off kingdoms.

My father was more distant, busier in a professional sense. Even though my mother earned a degree in counseling and taught university courses in later life, it was his work that put bread on the table. He was a professor at nearby St. John's, sold bonds to farmers on the side, got elected to the school board and eventually became a college administrator and president at small Catholic schools around the country. That accounts for the hectic moving we did during the decades of the '70s and '80s. He started off as a dashing professor of political philosophy — his favorite domain the classics of Greece and Rome — and ended up as a polished administrator raising large donations under the abstraction of "a quality education." It didn't make such a tight bond with us kids, but he saw to it that nine of his own made it through to a college degree, a legacy he believed in with all his heart.

In my mind I see the early years in my parent's home in black and white, like old television footage: movements all a little quick, Chaplinesque, not much self-consciousness. Plow ahead, that's all. By the time I came along, there was plenty of forward momentum. It didn't take long to realize I was to the rear of a sizeable train. All signals pointed to maintaining the established order: strong engines pulled, plenty of hands aboard. My only constraint was to sit back in notable obscurity, identity already determined — just another Henry — knowing we wouldn't be derailed or run out of fuel.

If ever I needed to impress friends, I marched them to the addition at Madison Elementary where, etched in St. Cloud granite on a wall-sized plaque, my father's name appeared: "Chairman of the School Board, 1963." Here was an engine pulling out front. I traced my fingers along sunken script trying to decipher, as if by Braille, exactly what this said about me. My nose probably wrinkled as I tossed my head. "See," I decided, "my father is a very important person, just like me." I kept the secret until I could achieve maximum effect. "He is the mayor of St. Cloud, you know." It was a part-time position, more stress than prestige, but it kept me from harm's way as untested minds measured it against the concept of ultimate authority. After a minute or so, attention was back on little-boy things: racing bikes, seeing who held breath the longest, arguing how many times their body-weight ants carry. But fathers carry weight, too: not so much in the immediacy of tied shoes, full tummies, as in the understanding of what to believe about ourselves beyond home.

* * *

My parents are part of a cohort which has been called (self-servingly perhaps) America's "greatest generation." I am no authority on greatness but I do admire the incredible distance that generation traveled: from small towns and modest homes, many without electricity, to world supremacy and a level of material comfort unknown to humankind. The United States got carried a long way on their backs, not to mention all those children — the Baby Boom another remarkable fact of American history. My parents, like the rest, pushed ahead undeterred, optimistic, faithful; or perhaps, as seems plain, completely unable to help themselves.

Recently, in reading through stacks of old correspondence written just prior my parent's wedding, I was struck by two things: the intensity and immediacy of their love for each other, how deep love always seems so precious, so new, so entirely here and now. And also, by their idealism, fueled by a hopefulness in the Catholic Church and a conviction that after a Depression and World War, society needed important change. This was a vital bearing in my parent's outlook, a significant part of their mutual attraction. They believed the world capable of immense and positive change, that lives lived according to principle were crucial steps in that direction. Furtive missives hurled back and forth from Dakota to Chicago, sometimes twice a day, explicating their understanding of Church teachings or projecting a path forward. Love, their wrinkled script shows, was foremost, but strong ideals filled their sails too. They pressed the two parts together and made a family.

I have never heard much about how the optimism and idealism of America's "greatest generation" fueled the eventual outpouring of activism during the 1960s. Yes, there is credit given for the manufacture of babies, but not much in terms of transmitting values, ideals or optimism which undergirded those eventually taking to the streets. Yet, it did not happen by accident. Communism, fascism and capitalism, the Marshall Plan, Korea and Sputnik — big ideas were on the table during the Baby Boom era. The growth of colleges and universities, not to mention elementary and secondary schools, exploded along with suburbs and the automobile. Education was being held up as a fundamental public good; Americans united as never before around the importance of children learning as the key to our future. And learn they did, in my opinion more than is commonly understood, from their first teachers. The '60s were an optimistic time, laden with ideals and a desire for positive change, inspiring a fully engaged generation compared to the civic apathy which governs our present.

My parents were not perfect. Over years, my father attached himself to work, spending long hours at the office or on the road promoting a new project. His intellectual qualities became a refuge from the messy world of family and he withdrew, leaving my mother to handle the sizeable emotional burdens for both of them. On her end, my mother developed a kind of cheerful, nattering distractedness. Busy with a million things, she threw herself into home and family and never took the time for her deepest interests or dreams. Their youthful love and optimism wore down against the realities of raising a large family, building careers, and spending a lifetime with someone as imperfect as themselves.

Parents take the blame when things go dreadfully wrong but fade easily into the background, as if it were completely natural, when a child turns up who clubs home runs, plays concertos or reinterprets Freud. What is not readily appreciated is how improvised their role is as a child's first teacher. How little parents actually prepare mentally, emotionally, intellectually for their job, but take it up as they go and end up exactly similar to or consciously different from the ones who raised them. There is a naturalness and a ubiquity to learning and teaching which does not call attention to itself — nowhere is this more true than in parenting. We want the best possible for the job but expend exactly zero as a society making sure that it happens. The fundamental importance of us each being a learner and a teacher emerges long before a child ever enters the world, not to mention their first classroom.

As teachers, my parents gave me a double-dose of faith in learning as the best route forward, and I took it up, despite occasional bouts of kicking and screaming. I sat for lessons in the back of some crowded class, talented and talkative older students seated up front. My mother instructed on romantic themes, taken by literature, art, aesthetics, and in times of trouble was always a soft place to land. My father taught more about backbone, order and discipline, a believer in the classical ideals of reason, social progress and civic duty. Education had propelled their own lives forward as a cannon-shot, overtaking the material abundance of their parents, inspiring hope for the lives of their children. Each did it with zest, juggling as much as playing the seasoned ringmaster. Underneath the circus tent the Henry's inhabited, there was a ton of everything — craziness, disputes, a religion, written and unwritten rules, teasing, joy, adventure — and also, the expectation that education, more than anything, was essential. It was what my parents left the house to do every day, along with all of my brothers and sisters. As professors of the Baby Boom, in public and private, they were incredibly adept, and I learned from them to feel at home in the world or heading out to school.

picture a thousand stories

At my Wisconsin farm I have a picture of our family from 1961: a Christmas shot, black and white, carefully composed in our St. Cloud home. I'm not sure it's 1961; only that sizes of siblings and me suggests it. I am barely a toddler, my pants probably full as I look attentively, like everyone, at the camera. Dropped from the dam in 1960, I would still be swaddled if it were that year; even more independent, able to stand, if shot in '62. The next youngest, Rebecca, holds a doll, and it is obvious from her arm-lock and bemused certitude that she has no intention of letting go. 1961 puts her at just over three; an age ripe for relationship. My mother, looking alert and content, sits forward faintly touching her — she who ended up resembling her most — flanked by children ascending head-over-head like steps of a pyramid to the governing figure of my father, holding me confident.

Something struck me about this photo, so I plucked it from a box, tacked it on my bathroom wall where I have studied it over months while pursuing important business: trying to write a book. The picture has become a kind of doorway, an entrance and meditation on the world of memory and meaning: how we create stories from the stuff of past living. It has also renewed my appreciation for the miracle of family. I love the captured expression on each face, personas revealing with disarming sincerity the people they actually became. That, and the truth of this being my first life, hoisted high on shoulders or getting trampled down below, always one of a multitude, a gangly sense of "manyness" at work inside me. To hear our family's whole number makes it seem unruly, impossible, but to see it plain in a photo like this, well, there we are, frozen, under complete control, reduced to a quick inventory. That softens edges, makes it more manageable, except that, as was usually the case, *we are still not all there.*

Tiny Rebecca, alone, squeezing the life out of her "Curly Miss LaPousse," makes this shot a premonition. Two years ago, at age 44, she was blessed with the baby she always wanted and now treasures, singing to like a blue-eyed doll. She has kept up more relationships than anyone. Mary, next to her, grips with knuckled determination the arm of my mother's chair, chest puffed, seemingly over-eager to get on with life, playing the obedient warrior. She ploughed her way forward to a busy government career, half-juggling, half-carrying her load, mother of an exhausting two herself. Susanna, behind her, a middle kid, looks slightly bored if not put off by the fuss. She stands a little apart — would partially obscure her older sister if completely aligned — and looks sheepish about her outfit, as if she might be happier in another room drawing or reading or painting. And so, over years, she has. Above her, Paula shows no fear or consternation; she seems to be gazing right through the photographer's lens, laser-like, as in "Would everyone just follow the directions, please!" She became the family epidemiologist. The girls are in dresses — two calicos, Susanna's jumper suit, and Becky's princess outfit — made by my mother, and wear saddle shoes, black and white with white laces. Maybe I love that most of all; that era of homemade, hand-done, the one-size-that-didn't-fit-all.

Manning the right flank, my brother Mike, with heine-cut and bow-tie, is the only one with hands in pockets as he beams a mischievous smile. Why is he so pleased? He has an air of invitation, like, "What'll it be? Cards? Tag? Cap guns?" Steven, in the middle, wears a white shirt, candy-striped tie and appears more taken by gravity, hands behind, hair combed over the top, shoulders rolled back; he looks to be biting his tongue in compliance with someone's great expectations. Amazing that he never landed in the military. Anne, the eldest, lurks above, appearing most comfortable; generous curly hair and a stretch sweater reveal the onset of puberty, perhaps even, some coming to terms with her secondary responsibility for this lively band of unknowns. She seems to understand there will always be work here.

Or maybe it's my image that makes this such a telling shot — isn't it our own face we examine foremost? Pulled in close to my father's chest, I have a look of pure wonder: eyes wide, mouth ajar from my index finger, red Christmas overalls (my mother sewed these too) bunched and stretched trying to cover a lumpy boy-body. Alert, curious, I may have just finished wriggling, the last piece of the photographer's puzzle, but I nevertheless hold a privileged position and relish it: higher than others, my heart and my father's never pressed so close. For awhile, I am pampered by the hazards of being the baby of the family.

In truth, what makes this photograph such a grand entrance is all of these things: each of us, the whole family, most especially the one clearly missing — younger brother John born in '63 — who might end up, if rank order follows, as last to tell a variation of our story. Because in the end, that is what stays with me about this picture and, to a large degree, my family and the crazy life we've fed upon. It's the stories; the act of narrative. Not just what they are by themselves, specifically — though that too; but how they form an indispensable loom we work our awareness on. The sheer fact that narratives work, that we return to them again and again, especially because there are manifold versions and a million ways to tell them. Recalled at any hour, from any distance, with any level of detachment, emotion, accuracy or deceit, used to argue, convince, cajole, refute, confuse, amuse or just to hold onto because in some ultimate sense — like family and breath itself — they're all we've got.

* * *

We used to hunt agates. Unlike regular hunting, agates don't require weapons or special gear, just a righteous stride and steady gaze. That's something we were good at. Looking straight down, walking miles of dirt road on long, limber legs, past haunted houses and cow pasture, rooting out rocks, kicking mulishly at dirt-clods. Every once in a while we'd pull one up with a smooth, glassy surface, bands of translucent color waving deeply toward the center, sometimes all the way through. We spit on them, rubbed to make sure they were "keepers"; everyone looked and appraised value before we dropped it in a sack for later, when we spread them on a bed or table, replaying as best we could who found what and where. This was up at our cottage, what we call "the old lake," Lake Nokay or Lake Nokasippi. It's on a feeder chain that fills the Mississippi. We claimed if you paddled for a couple days you could make Little Falls; Sauk Rapids in a week; St. Louis, well, she's out there. Though we always lugged our way by automobile — about two hours — riding the *grande dame*, Old Bessy, a white war-horse Fairlane station-wagon with subdued fins and a square back. She wasn't a boat but could have been if she ever flipped in a pond with how we crammed her generous holds.

My father located the old farm house by Brainerd in the late-fifties. It was a natural for our tribe bursting its teepee but otherwise not much to talk a round about: two bedrooms, a living room, a kitchen with an old cook-stove and a screened porch which barely kept us dry in a downpour. The place had that smell — damp cellar mixed with an ancient soft decay in every board and inch of plaster — and was one of about a dozen equally modest cabins clustered on the north bluff of an often weed-choked basin. Not luxury by any means. The lake was small; you could shout someone back from across the water. A long, steep hill led down to the shore and our improvised stairway made of rickety oak-branch was constantly rotting, in need of repair.

Yet somehow, the old lake worked its way under our skin until it became a kind of Genesis for us; and also, given how we sang around campfires, our Book of Psalms. From our time there comes a spiral of stories, songs and legends, lists of friends and neighbors, accounts of bravery or foolishness, memories of charmed escapes and natural invention. Singing a flaming birthday cake to the table, watching a storm's lightning stabs over the water, how my father used to insist on burning the hillside, which meant brigades of youth hauling sloppy buckets of water for hours. We laughed, we swam, we went to the rural parish church on Sunday mornings. Mike once hooked a lake gull while casting; Steve, a snapping turtle. When black-and-white splotched cows escaped the pasture fence waddling into our yard one afternoon, I was overcome by their girth or grace or gaze and fainted cold on the porch. And so on, ratcheting down the iron pump-handle to draw water, bathing children on the lawn in a round washtub, young John floating face down near the shore looking for a lost truck. It started small canvass, then cascaded into master tableau — pontoon fishing with neighbors, raccoons retreating to the dock end with watermelon rinds, coming home from summer with tanned bodies and slightly deeper voices. We grew up atom by atom, in common orbit, filling peanut-butter jars with agates.

And every year, when Labor Day came, it was time to pack and go home. This was a mixed blessing. Older kids generally favored returning to friends and a familiar neighborhood. Younger ones perhaps secretly regretted such a separation and loss of freedom as school brought with it — at least for part of an afternoon. Before we could crush ourselves into Old Bessy though, we'd have to spend the morning doing chores and closing up. It meant sweeping the floors, baiting mouse-traps, draining water back, tossing moth balls around, wiping the fridge, looking under every bed, sofa and chair and going through that place like a platoon vacating a barracks.

The year I'm reminded of, we had finished by noon of Labor Day, padlocked the heavy wood door, heard the screen's screeching slam, then scrunched together in the wagon to discuss the expected "limit" Dad would allow at Dairy Queen on the way home. We backed out, motoring slowly along the rutted road whose grass strip made a familiar brushing sound on our under-carriage. Bessy lifted and sagged through dips and washouts, forded puddles, chugged hills. Why she put up with heaps of abuse and overwork I will never know; my mother up front watched out, eyes alert, turning as she would, to count heads. One, two, three, four, five, six, seven, eight. Eight. But not nine. "Oh my gosh, is that right? For crying out loud, we're missing someone!" At first murmurs of disbelief, then recounts, near alarm and a kind of somber undertone about what might have happened — but never did we get nine. We went clear to the inlet that day before realizing we lacked one of our essentials — John, the baby, the absence in that photo.

"Where was he last?" My father's heightened voice revealed that this was no gag or artifice. No one really knew. The out-house? At the neighbors? Down by the lake? We fished a turn-around and sped Bessy back the way she came, more grass thrashing, water sprays and seat-clearing bumps than previous. Four doors sprang open as we rolled to a stop, young legs speeding off in several coordinated directions. In the end, we were surprised, though not especially troubled, by the depth of depravity the truth revealed: young John had simply been padlocked in the cabin, left with our other gear to winter-over. Apparently, if you weren't large or assertive and if you weren't easily carried by the crowd, you might just get left behind. After initial despair, he had adjusted; we found him comfortably barricaded in a bedroom with picture book and a box of graham crackers, about halfway through each. My father plucked him up and carried him out as if the place were burning; fresh tears began to flow quenching any flames.

It doesn't need sentimentalizing but this story comes up regularly when we talk old lake, sprawling family, cars we've owned, how Mom held it together one way — Dad the other, or why John likes to read so much. Some narratives carry extra weight and have the face to cut across several fields at once. I wish I could stretch this one further, hold that it influenced my decision to go into teaching. That way back I developed a sense of wanting to help, to be a "catcher in the rye" for lost youngsters. It's understandable to believe in such things: epiphanies around which wagons can be circled as defining who we are and how we got there. Unfortunately, like many contemporary presumptions, that would be an oversimplification, a "no child left behind" trope not unlike one already perpetrated on the American public.

An aptitude for learning, our essential character, coming into values — these are built slowly, steadily over time through relationship, exposure to a rich environment, watching others, taking small steps, gauging results and moving forward. A complete version of what makes us who we are is not easy to come by; nor are there perfect outcomes. We accumulate experience and decide later what it means; even then the story is subject to alteration, reinterpretation. And in the real world, children get left behind everyday, as do others, whether elderly, sick or just unremarkable. Not many leap to their defense or selflessly commit to a life of service because of it. In that, I am not much different from the world that made me.

The lesson — if narratives need such things — is simpler, less extra-ordinary, and perhaps in a way, more universal: It's possible to have too many children, and there are times when I think we do. But not so memories, agates or gateways into a story. These refuse to grow up and die, even when born from an absence in an old photograph.

no child's story left behind

At the core of narrative, like "old lake" stories, are wooly memories which sporadically surface and startle me: long forgotten trips to an aunt's convent for Easter egg decorating, a yellow-tipped blue flame deep within our basement furnace, goofy faces, oddly comforting, from a first grade class photo. Wooly as in not taken out often or used. It also suggests moth-eaten, rough, like artifacts long-buried — damp, diminished — but still capable of reviving a forgotten afternoon. Whatever basis they have in fact, memories rearrange themselves to fit current needs and fashion, a definite hazard for trying to land the truth. The task thus, is one of careful detachment: drawing out valuable substance from rich and varied material while keeping alert to issues of forgery. It would seem there is inherent kinship in the work of writing and being a teacher.

I have this vague memory about playing outside in St. Cloud. I pretend to be a deer, in fact two or three of us were an entire family. We made a protected place to lay down, had a browse area in the bushes and crawled around on fours, it feels like, all afternoon. The cool thing was, we didn't really talk. We were deer and thus made deer noises, kind of cooing, affectionate sounds, genuinely caring for each other with nuzzles, a working out of family intimacy I had no exposure to.

One time we were pawing grass out front and practically got run over. This is wooly, too. My brother Mike, the unenviable middle kid, comes charging through the yard whooping and hollering, his best friend executing a bob-sled push on a wagon between them filled with trays, boxes, balloons and bright packages. "Carnival!" They yell. "Don't miss it!" This was the terminus of a block-long procession, which picked up steam all down 28th Avenue — as well as a decent number of neighbor kids, intrigued and curious. Heine's predominated back then, a super-short buzz-cut. I see a dozen or so dope-eared boys in longish blue-jean shorts, and just a few pony-tailed girls in T-shirts standing around like hicks at a small-town dance.

They set up our "boxes and boards" — local parlance for painted planks and slotted wood frames from which you could freely construct a pretty major outfit — and soon were charging pennies or nickels over the counter for chance games and skill contests. Drop a rubber ball in a maze and see what you win. Throw darts at balloons hiding numbers. Toss rings at Coke bottles. Prizes were generally Tootsie Rolls, suckers and gum, or straight cash, though I remember Mike sent away to television once and got back an entire kit, complete with legitimate gifts like signed celebrity photos and small stuffed animals. He and buddy Bob did a really big carnival on that one — even put up signs. They were to send back profits which got donated to a cause like March of Dimes. That part of it I'm not sure got done fully. Mike walked around after like a banker ready to underwrite the next big thing, if anyone besides him had a concept.

I'm not sure how his childhood fascination converted itself into something larger — and more painful: what lit the fuse on his lifetime love of money, big ideas and gambling. Mike invariably had an interest simmering on the stove — stamp collecting, unusual diets, conspiracy theories — and if it had a money angle to it, so much the more alluring. Sitting on the curb outside supermarkets, he would search rolls of coins bought from the cashier hoping to find feather-back pennies, buffalo nickels or mercury dimes, which he then referenced and fit neatly into slots in blue coin albums. He had thorough admiration for the world of American capitalism where you are given immediate feedback, painful or ecstatic, as to the success of your latest venture.

There's probably a person in every American family not unlike Mike. Maybe a little of him in everyone, including me. I don't see how standing there on all fours like a deer as he raced past with a carnival wagon is far off from his own stabs at knowing the world. We all throw ideas and dreams at a wall and see which ones we can make stick. Kids maybe do it more often. It's a learning process; an instinct which is pure, elemental and profound. It happens in small and large ways every day — from discovering how to keep parents at bay to mastering the uses of a rubber band. Inevitably, as we mature, we're directed into more predictable, standardized arenas, shot down for being naïve or impractical. No more monsters on the front lawn; believing in super-human powers as a teenager won't do. Less sticks, there's not much joy or abandon: fear of ridicule or being different win out. We put away improvised maps and treasure clues, settle down to life as it conventionally happens: go to school, get a job, make dinner, watch T.V., live for the weekend. I hope this never happens to me. And Mike, I know it will never happen to him. Bless his heart for not getting down on possibilities or his methodology. Just the other day he shrugged off a stock decline, told me matter-of-fact the market was going up 30 percent in six weeks — before crashing worse than the Depression for a decade.

* * *

My fuse got lit as a youngster, too; though in a way diametrically oppo-site to the allure of making money. When I was eight, I decided to write. This wasn't well thought out. I didn't know enough to romanticize the lifestyle: to believe in a regular table at the Café Montparnasse where I could sip absinthe and roar with literary lions past midnight. Nor did I labor under illusions of uniqueness or irreplaceability: eight siblings made me realize a credible version is always at hand should a red-faced adult stand over you asking what just happened. I do admit though, writing may have been an effort to bring clarity to ideas which never received a full hearing at home. Attention spans in our family were notoriously brittle, with children dashing, phones ringing, music blaring, disputes erupting. There just wasn't much focus or lucidity brought to bear. A sensitive person might go crazy under such conditions; having the eighth voice up from the bottom meant even less in terms of recognition and value.

Back then, my mother bought "Big Chief" tablets of notepaper by the dozen. On the cover, a depiction of a Native American stared out in sympathetic earth tones — long hair, stoic features, feather headdress. It felt adventurous to see what horizons I might look across or smoke signals send up. I traced around my hands, smeared pencil into solid hues then etched coins in it; or filled pages with numbers or letters or words, an illeg-ible Peter Francis Henry written over and over. Even in a household as chaotic as ours, there was time enough for one kid to explore recesses in his mind. Not that there was genius involved making a decent sized mess: filling sheets, tearing out, crumpling, then imagining basketball again, arcing jump-shots at a trash can across the room.

In third grade we set to learning penmanship. Mrs. Connors had this special paper, extra space between solid lines so a dotted one could run the middle, depicting half-way. We made big "A" and small one; large "B" and junior "b", etc. She compelled us to write strings of letters, all little "s's" across the row. It seemed most small letters didn't make it past the dotted line, though I surprised myself arranging tall ones, like "f" and "k" and connecting them to create funny words. I didn't get hooked by phonics or even writing just for practice; to me it mattered more what lurked beyond, what they pointed at. The process is remarkable though: an aptitude for tiny marks intensifies as you invest in them, grow older, until eventually they detach from the page and fly as tiny arrows, piercing those hunched over them.

My first sneaky efforts at composition conform to the declaration "Write what you know." I attempted a book about the Minnesota Vikings 1967 football season. I stapled notebook paper, compiled records, wrote headlines and drew pictures of exceptional plays, which ended up resembling awkward monsters each falling in their own direction. Everything was going swimmingly. The Vikes rolled to a division crown behind the "Purple People Eaters" and Joe Kapp. Sadly however, the project crashed in the fourth quarter of their playoff game with San Francisco. Dave Osborne, trusty soldier of a back, fumbled and the 49ers later got a touchdown. The last sentence reads: "Osborne fumbled the ball. The Vikings lost their season is over." (I couldn't draw grammar right either.) I stapled on a new cover, an oblong fumble helped off the page with swooshes. My project, no longer an epic and as oblivious as I was to its possible tragic implications, was shelved. I went back to other noble boy pursuits: playing hockey, racing *Hot Wheels* around a plastic orange track, running away with pretty girl's hats.

Another early attempt failed too. I remember hearing that when Mark Twain created Tom Sawyer, that the character was a composite of various real-life people. That seemed wise. All I had to do was combine my roster of buddies into one, bigger than life, he-did-everything kind of kid. So I took names of friends, grabbed a couple letters each and came up with: *Jerry Moutzman.* Jerry was going to be a modern Tom Sawyer — painting garages in mud, stealing apples, shoplifting key chains, the whole gamut of nefarious goings-on I knew about. Scrupulous, though not particularly circumspect, I avoided using my own letters in Jerry's name so that I would not be associated in any way with activities in my book. People were going to read it, you know. Maybe even adults.

Unhappily, Jerry's story never was completed. In a way, aside from an initial page and a half, it never got started. As a teacher, I wonder what kept me from completing more of it. At the time, I knew almost nothing about constructing narrative, telling a story: how quotes are used, character developed, how essential are detail and vocabulary. I knew little about writing but was certain about one thing: there was plenty of material growing up in a small-town during the kid-laden decade of the '60s. This had me believing I possessed everything I needed, never mind an unvaccinated urge to make sense of it somehow, which was beginning to show signs of sticking around.

What strikes me about this is the little boy alone in the living room working with a Big Chief tablet. How children don't know if they can or can't, if they are or aren't writers or singers or athletes. What they throw at the wall just sits there most of the afternoon as child's play and then is forgotten. It is always other people, usually adults, who reveal to them the possibility in play and especially, in themselves. I am not certain anyone ever peaked over my shoulder, heard my big idea of writing a book; or if I explained what I did care about, what fascinated me.

I'm not looking for sympathy or excuses, but only want to highlight an important fact: the early aspirations and activities of children are sacred. These are unwitting expressions of what fulfills the little being trying to emerge from inside the shell. They are crucial indications of direction and value. All it takes is time from a caring, knowledgeable person, perhaps a little guidance, and the child realizes it is a good path, one they can explore and develop over a lifetime. It also makes this work, whether teaching or parenting or just being with a kid, sacred. Sacred because it is so much more than ourselves — beyond our knowing — and has repercussions out there ricocheting in the universe. It is a very simple thing, too. So powerfully simple. We literally create each other's talent and interests, or at least draw them out and make them real, by extending time toward another person and what they are doing. And yet, in the context of contemporary America, in our frenzied embrace of productivity and efficiency as supreme values, it is exceptionally difficult to achieve.

I am not alone in suggesting that this makes schools more crucial than ever to development in young people. It would be nice if ideal families produced well-adjusted children motivated to learn, but as in our family's case — with loving parents, lively siblings and financial stability — it isn't always possible. Some kids are destined to struggle. Under even the best circumstances children still undergo basic processes: the experience of loss, needing and wanting love, questioning their identity.

Today, with so many fragmented homes and overworked adults, countless kids practically raise themselves from a very young age. In increasing numbers, they come to school with large gaps in their lives, their identity and being. Educational facilities are required to prepare for a population on the edge, frequently administering first aid, first comfort, first care. What most Americans do not fundamentally "get" about contemporary schooling is that it is not simply a matter of adding information and skills to a willing participant. There are serious obstacles holding students back, messy circumstances which have more authority over them than educators ever will. Our schools' most vital obligation today is often as much about providing emotional and developmental triage as in instructing the basics. More than ever, public schools have to stand in as the caring adult beside a youngster, helping him or her to see value and hope in what they are doing.

Richard LaVoie, a special education teacher from Boston, has written about thinking of students in terms of the number of "poker chips" they possess as a result of experiences within their family of origin. Unlike real poker, the chips here represent the relative wealth of human connection each child has had; the state of their self-concept and personal confidence after growing up in a careful or careless environment. Like everywhere in America, there are some very well-off children carrying stacks of chips; there are also those less fortunate — afflicted by abuse, neglect, a lack of basic skills — who carry next to nothing. Those with a ton learn how to protect, build and marshal their store for their benefit; they have few problems in learning, development and making a secure life for themselves. Those with very little believe they have nothing to lose by acting out or giving up on people or education; a sense of scarcity and desperation guides their choices, which narrow down as they age. This is not simply a matter of class or economics — though it's foolish to imagine that traditional wealth plays no role. Nor does it mean youngsters can't overcome great odds or that being upper-class precludes having problems; there are plenty of each. What it does mean is that we need to consider the reality of each student individually, learn their particular story and set up meaningful ladders toward their own kind of progress.

We all come to the world through the experience of being a child. Everyone has a set of wooly memories which get strung together into a storyline...the first tentative steps on a stage with others. There is a growing person in there, a young star's dressing-room decked out with dreams, loves, fears and disappointments. Look at their work: innocent doodling along borders, the uncertain way they wade out into assertions of difference, clandestine routes used to avoid revealing the truth. They need someone to see that, to understand and know how to work with them on valuing their story, dressing it out as a means to a better end. My own upbringing was not ideal in that, with such a large family, I learned to slide by without attention, my own needs and projects frequently hidden or ignored. Perhaps though, this is just the right edge with which to examine these other worlds carefully now; in a way I would have wished for myself at that age.

I know from experience on both sides of the equation that nothing assists the process of growing up more than a wise person overseeing development, genuinely appreciating who you are, where you are at. In my case, I was blessed with many caring, talented instructors who took notice and worked hard to ensure my path was a good one. They are my sacred guides, along with my parents, to whom I owe so much gratitude;

people whose quiet belief in children's lives have made all the difference.

Mrs. Smith, my first-grade teacher, was a woman truly blessed with wonderful qualities. She taught us the alphabet in joyous song, how to read, count, and unfurl and nap on rugs after milk in the afternoon. She put on the best one-person rendition of *Brer Rabbit* ever performed in elementary school. She loved children; she loved her work. Years later when I was in college, she wrote from retirement, explaining how much she enjoyed teaching me as a youngster — there at the bottom of the page, the same smiley face that used to be on all my early projects and papers. If only I could find her now and show her this. Imagine the stars I could get!

Mr. Frantee, in that very same school, was a top gym teacher. I remember how periods began with a phonograph recording of "Chicken Fat," a musical callisthenic program that got us stretching, marching, doing push-ups, sit-ups and rolling on our backs, Mr. Frantee in the background exhorting or adjusting or modeling like Robert Preston in *The Music Man*. One of his teeth was gold, but otherwise he looked just like a kid — little cushion of hair, reddened cheeks, the gleam of play in his eyes. He loved being vocal, getting to the right word in a sentence, sending it sailing across the gym to echo in our minds for all time, especially names: "Moutzman! What are you doing?"

Mrs. Nucci, a short heavy-set sixth-grade teacher I had in South Bend, never said "wrong" or "incorrect" or "no," but simply smiled in front of the class, waiting for one more answer, one more hand to go up, the chance to shake her head in glowing confirmation of what she was looking for. She was a master teacher, somewhere near 60, secure in her methods and approach. Tough boys talked about how she "rolled" down the hallway, a giant bowling ball, but none of us ever got away from her hugs after school, and we had plants and pets and projects on the windowsills and cabinets from September into June.

In eighth grade, I had Mr. Hugo in language arts. He asked for, and generally received, a page of writing to be turned in on Mondays, Wednesdays and Fridays. Not a big deal, because you had the class period to do it; or, you could write it before-hand and use class to continue in the workbook. He was a portly man, middle aged, with red bushy hair and a cherub's face who looked like he spent evenings in a cardigan, sipping sherry, smoking from a pipe. I remember being quite startled one day when, after I turned in my assignment, he burst out laughing in a voice that rolled over and over itself as if heading downhill out of control. I wrote that paper only five minutes before; now here it was a source of amusement in a relative stranger. That felt odd, even shocking. In polite terms, adults were to be avoided; they mostly invoked limits or consequences, not to imagine that we might write something that makes them climb down off their pedestal in fits of hilarity.

Mr. Burns was a history teacher in Vermont. Every bit a Scot, sandy hair flowing behind a balding pate and twinkling smile, he loved language, ornate and crafty. He was quick with a story, usually from American history about Franklin, Jefferson, Monroe, Burr, et al, but also possibly the local paper whose more bizarre matters struck his fancy. He held the paper in his hand, threw on a pair of bifocals, pausing now and again to make his points, his tummy slightly slumped in silhouette. I loved his upbeat verbal style, constant search for irony, the serene stability he represented in a chaotic, careless environment. Writing assignments sought our reactions; exams meant college-like 'Blue Books' where we created dialogues, wrote mock journals in the voice of an Andrew Jackson or Teddy Roosevelt. It was the first time I slowed down to formulate words into arguments and coherent positions, not just flights of fancy or entertaining vignettes as in junior high. We threw serious stuff at the wall, and to my surprise, most of it stuck.

* * *

In ninth grade, I learned my family would be moving for the fourth time in six years, leaving Minnesota for Vermont. Like every nay-saying adolescent, this seemed unbearable. My natural response was to retreat inside, realizing that I would have to bear this burden alone. At 16, family is no use. In a way, a big way actually, this move was about loss. Loss and coming of age. Alone. Very alone. To make sense of it, I turned to poetry, though at the time I had no idea why. In my room late at night, I fidgeted through possessions, listened to music and wrote little rhyming couplets about how I saw things: why people acted like they did, how false were some fronts, what really mattered in the hearts of human beings. Looking back now I can make the detached assessment of an English teacher: Is this bad poetry? Yes. Very bad. Closer to nursery rhymes than Dylan Thomas. But the urge to write was not bad; it was curative and may have saved my life.

Some of us walk around out here, taking in experiences, feelings, people and, because our gyroscope doesn't ground us, need an opening to understand and sort them. Only after writing do they make sense: life counts up right, emotions find their basin to soak in. Without a narrative assembly we would be stuck in a continuously infinite experience, a kind of acid trip that never winnows down or tracks back to lucidity. I have a hunch that most people do this verbally, or at least, I get stuck next to ones that do. We capable listeners take the brunt of their mental tidying up, though it is for a good cause I suppose: sanity. We're content to take this chaotic world in stride, even its most bombastic inhabitants, sorting it out later when no one's around. That's when it makes the most sense anyway.

This same tendency, to have writing provide some final structure, exists in journals I have kept semi-faithfully since high school. Here I assembled consistently underdeveloped entries, sometimes enticing but usually vague bits and drams of life held up to momentary scrutiny, written flat, without the aid of intervening perspective:

> Friday night with the Blais and Mace was something else. Saturday was intrinsically beautiful, the skiing at Red Rocks Park. Sunday has faded slowly from view. So now I sit at my desk. To say there is no melancholy would be a half-truth. It is one of pain and alienation, though. A long time ago, I felt none of this. I have been conditioned; I live in Vermont.

What this meant is not clear; how it added lucidity to my stumbly existence back then baffles me. I had an intense need to know who I was at the core — that there really was a core — and writing provided that: it became the home base I didn't necessarily have in a chaotic family.

This needing to write as an internal process is what Howard Gardner, the Harvard learning style specialist, calls being an "intra-personal" learner, someone who maps such things with enough poignancy that others find it helpful in understanding their own process. In my case, it is the feeling during the moment of creation which gives it such allure: blissful abandon in which time, identity, even surroundings are temporarily gone. The experience feels genuinely therapeutic, though it might be a kind of disease if you factor in deepest desires for the finished product. Somehow an ego gets involved and hijacks the process. That delightful act of creation which nails the world precisely suddenly mushrooms to unmanageability, trumping concern for basic needs: food, rest, companionship. It's not unlike my brother Mike all over again, all the way to the hard money edge. "I've got it figured; I know how this works; I absolutely do. Just one other thing…" The mind falls in love with its chosen object of affection, a carnival, a coin-collection, the perfect way to frame a story, believing that with just the right touch, it's only moments away from striking it big.

* * *

Despite any difference in purpose or intention, writers — famous ones as well as novices trying to gain a foot-hold — essentially do a similar thing. It is the quality of attention that unites them; that need I felt as a boy to follow an idea despite, or because of, the chaos which enveloped me. The intention is to make meaning from scraps of existence which often feel disconnected, confused, incoherent. A lifetime of small and large matters gather at their feet, impede movement, unless they erect a kind of framework or spinal column upon which these can be purposefully strapped. Long years of awkwardness or delight or ignorance arrange themselves so that a larger truth can take their place — as if this was dependent all along upon wooly details forming a crucial base.

I am fascinated by this process, bow before the essential connectedness of these efforts. Written stories, after all, form the basis of most major religions. Our very history and destiny is woven from the golden thread of narrative: coherence and meaning plucked like jewels from the wash of everyday life. This, too, is sacred work. As in spending time with children, writing means sending out a small piece of humanity to the universe, hoping that it inspires, ricochets, reverberates across a broad spectrum of souls until touching down in its own place of home. It is a form of magic, an enchantment, a sort of unintended cult — a pursuit at once ubiquitous and communal, as well as solitary and private. Readers lose themselves as surely as the writer does, willingly dipping themselves into the same pool of timeless mirth, self-forgetfulness; emerging, they find themselves unusually refreshed, alert to opportunities for consciousness.

Remarkable too, that writing is so basic. No fancy technology can increase your insight, no amount of money or fame improves the quality of your encounter with its demands. It isn't about age or race or sex or ethnicity or even religion. In the end, it is about an ability to see everything, including yourself, exactly like it is: naked, inert, alone, the flab and moles and possible attractions. And perhaps especially at the beginning, remembering that this is how you, and every being, came here: as single bodies with endless possibility. Then you dress this in a way which makes sense, devising connections and relationships so that the solitary in each of us becomes a kind of binding, drawing us together in a book.

* * *

Memory. Narrative. Teaching. I will admit to being taken by the past; how as time moves on we endeavor to keep it alive, seeking solid ground upon which we can pin understanding of what it meant. Teaching, and particularly writing, are about designing that space, confronting what is no longer here by using what is: being both generous and critical, following curiosity to discover more, or less, than imagined. Also, I need to acknowledge, that this process is as much a symbolic closing of the coffin-lid as the magic I referred to earlier. Bringing people and events back before us, we secure them like statues into an unchanging form, reduce them to an understandable husk of what they were so we can visualize a way beyond them. It's the best we can do; really, the best I can do. And I need remind myself not to be disappointed: resurrection by narrative always serves the living more than the dead.

Perhaps this is why that Christmas photo from 1961 has felt so important as I have sifted through my past. I realize that studying it carefully — exploring the wooly alley-ways of a young life coming forward — has helped me grasp something terribly important: namely, how many things changed unpredictably since I was first the little boy in my father's arms. How challenging would be my relationship with him, how I never really accepted my parent's Catholicism, how a simpler era in American society shattered into a million shards of complexity, how I watched as our family moved away repeatedly from home and friends, how even siblings drifted off to college one-by-one until I was left growing up alone with my brother John. With that photo as a starting point, I can pinpoint more than ever what things have gone unexpectedly lost in my life.

But I also see that as much as these things were given up or taken away, essential replacements rolled in underneath like some oceanic tide filling the void — as if we all possess an inner-sense of what makes for level. Thus I rejected a religion but kept a sense of the sacred in the way of writing and working with youngsters; American culture grew more complex and frenzied but only reinforced in me the importance of being stable, sticking to core values; friends vanished only to reappear in another state, wearing bigger grins, a different jersey; my large family moved out one-by-one but the sense of communion in a group never did. What stayed with me was always implicit, not explicit instruction. I lost the specific details but kept a general sense of what matters, what I needed to feel sustained, whole. And now it serves its purpose: even though both of my parents were teachers, nothing they ever told or taught me explicitly pointed me in the direction of being one myself. And yet, as students file into my class everyday, I feel oddly well prepared to intuit where they are at, what they need, how to go about this job of catching them into learning.

The belief that our children's lives will be secured once and for all if we just administer enough exams or force-feed them enough data is, for lack of a better word, wrong. Terribly wrong. We are reversing the formula of explicit and implicit knowing, forcing them to remember obscure facts while ignoring key teachings from their own life. And in the process we are undermining, if not rupturing, the one essential aspect of learning and being at school without which nothing positive can be realized: the delicate relationship between a child and a teacher.

If I know anything about the job of teaching it is just this: we learn far more from close study of our own lives than anything we pick up in class or from reading. This is the primary foundation of our being, in each of us our Holy Book. And it is here that the three arcs — my own past as a student, the lives of children, and learning to teach — intersect. Thus, it is absolutely essential to provide every youngster a chance to write and share their own story. To take the time to flesh out the main events, people and places that make a life unique, irreducible and allow them to share that with the world. It is the one indispensable subject at which they are expert and can readily teach others, becoming a teacher themselves.

I know it sounds simple, even obvious, but contemporary pressures from standards and endless achievement tests make it more difficult and more unlikely than ever. Teachers are being asked not to see students as unique human beings, but only as receptacles for facts and manipulators of formulas who will someday become an income and a daily work schedule, however mindless or dull.

We must resist this. Parents and teachers need only remember their own lives as youngsters — as students — to understand the importance of listening to and valuing the early inspirations of children. Time must be found for the creation of each story. This is more than an exercise for boosting self-esteem. Composers of narrative are rewarded by measure of the accuracy, depth and sincerity they bring to their account; it inures them to finding truth in themselves and the world. Ideally, this crosses over, keeps them vigilant to wring disingenuousness from important issues in their day. It reinforces that each of them is a worthy vessel capable of ushering important gifts into being. The little boy clinging to his father, a thousand ways lost growing up, rafting overcrowded toward unknown shores, now standing as an intrepid guide for youngsters facing the same journey. Ultimately, there is no shame acknowledging the truth of what happened to you in life. Nor any sure way to avoid it resurfacing as you plunge ahead attempting to forget. In fact, in most cases, telling it is the only effective way forward: going through, not around it. What is lost in the failure to relate or even understand a person's own life, is a grounded understanding of what it means to be a human being.

* * *

In St. Cloud, we flew kites. As with most things, we weren't artistic about it or cultured; we didn't start from scratch with sticks and sealing wax or try Japanese style. But we did bring a kind of organizational intensity which was impressive. Out in central Minnesota there can be quite a breeze, especially in Spring and Autumn when hemispheric weather patterns wriggle around, pulling and adjusting the covers of temperature and precipitation as they see fit. If you get a kite up into the main channel, high above tree line, it really fills up with thrust.

One (wooly) time, I remember we got a kite way out there. It started with just the usual kite in a kit and a couple balls of string but somehow turned into a project. Mike was there. Go figure. He went for more balls of string, then talked friends into it, neighbors, even a stray passer-by or two — one of those matches again between imagination and realities in the world. A little store was close by, and they were probably happy as anyone to see things get that far, the wrinkled lady bagging up roll after roll of white cotton string. Our kite's board of directors, on which the Henrys had a majority, were reluctant to allow young children to hold it for fear they would be swept away. (That would really catch us hell — everyone grounded except the unfortunate idiot who didn't let go and now floats somewhere in outer-space.) An Einstein in the neighborhood realized if we back-tied it to a tree, almost anyone could touch it without a huge personal risk. We watched it through binoculars and established teams on bike who circulated in distant neighborhoods downwind in case she broke free. We added more and more string. No one was sure what we were doing or why, only that it was a lot of fun to stand in our yard and realize we had a line out to the sky. Way out. Visible for miles. Over 20 balls of string. If God or the local airport approved of any of this, we didn't consider.

I took my turn. Mike passed me the line unevenly, like he was fighting some incredible force, his left arm straining it down to my little hand.

What a thrill! The thing bobbed and weaved and tugged, gave me the full flavor of nature's capricious ways. It just might take me with it, first here, then there — hang on! And I did, until the next in line claimed their turn. These operations were our family's specialty and usually based upon democratic principal. There was occasional selfishness or overzealous competition, but I know I was right about one thing: our backyard was as good a place to discover the world as any. In the grand scheme I understood that my junior existence didn't add up to a hill of beans. But I also knew, even in a large family, with as many twists and turns as that kite out there, that I did get a turn. To get a chance. To be put in, even in right field; to get one good throw at the carnival booth or just to hold this kite. Who really knows where small things might lead? And I realized instinctively, maybe purely for the first time, that whatever was holding me down in the world of the present, this other possibility, floating limitless above streets and people and problems, did exist. That in my neighborhood back then, all you needed to get there was family, some friends, a 50-cent kite, 27 balls of string, and perhaps if you were a particularly ponderous child like myself, a Big Chief tablet and pencil.

the odd couple

My routine in high school was to wake by alarm, drag-ass to the shower, throw clothes on, grab breakfast, then dance to the driveway where my Valiant waited, as well as a red-haired neighbor girl. I ran a small-time car pool. Five bucks a week got lifts for Red, a boy three houses up, Julia of a few streets over and Joey Bookchin, who lived in a completely different universe. By and large, the operation ran smooth (honk, honk) until the Bookchins, a New York Jewish enclave in a modest Burlington neighborhood where things typically ground to a halt. Joey was perpetually unprepared, caught by complete surprise and we waited for ten minutes sometimes in painful silence as he tore through the house, tossed his pack together, loved his Ma, struggled with an overcoat — what was he doing in there? Then he bounced out, tails untucked, toast in hand but eternally unflappable, disposed to see life in his zany, existential, post-modern way. Witty, urbane and self-consciously mature, the question was always: Is the world ready for Bookchin? — and not the reverse.

I never minded that Joey's pool account was constantly in arrears; it was a small price to pay for being forever enlarged. Joey's dad was Murray Bookchin, a famous anarchist who had written books; I'd never heard of him. I met Joey in *World Cultures* class in 10th grade. We had Mr. Meyers, another New York *emigre*; his wife was a pediatrician at the local hospital. He was a little out of his league (if not, mind) teaching sophomores, most of whom could give a rat's ass for "culture". Impeccable in suit, tie, tidy wire-rim glasses and well-managed hair, Meyers was serious and intellectual at an historical moment which called for humor and apathy. Only Bookchin and I appreciated his schtick; in fact, we bonded over it — Meyer's musings about human destiny, his suppositions about national foibles. We slowly got to know each other, exchanging smiles, nods, small talk, completely aware we were transgressing the rigid social boundaries of high school. I remember staying after on the last day to discuss Meyer's essay question. We were to create a culture from scratch and present their entire belief system: religion, mores, values and art. Meyers couldn't quite get over my exam, which included a drawing of how this new cultural group — half-fish, half-human — came to be. I had a rough-looking carp in silhouette on top of a naked woman near a river — no fig leaves — his one large eye seemingly aware there were outside observers. It was as uncouth as it was daring. From this fertile but sinful genesis emerged not only a wealth of unusual culture and iconography, but also an unlikely friendship.

* * *

If family is a first life — riding high on shoulders or being trampled down below — friends are a close second. Here we play more equal: pals in principle not of blood. They suit needs, challenge biases, teach what to appreciate and look out for. I had my own set of bosom buddies: in St. Cloud, Dave Mueller — a short, conventional neighbor who was easy-going but with troubled brothers himself. In South Bend where we moved in 1972, Jack Kintzal, a vibrant and action-loving amigo who thirsted for adventure and intrigue. Back in St. Cloud in junior high, Joe Meierhoffer, a super-friendly, always smiling and athletic-minded buddy — buddy who knew fishing, hunting and charming girls. And in Vermont, Bookchin, the wiry, curly-haired philosopher with glasses whose whole being was devoted to mannerisms, parody and incisive analysis about existence. My quixotic life is the sole relational context that will ever view these incongruous souls in the same plane. There was no way to realize it then, but they formed a kind of protective aura despite my miserable aloneness, mirrored changes I grew into and, while throwing me further out, kept me secure in a cocoon of intimate connection.

Family sets out a pattern, determines parts of what you become, but at a certain point stands back and has to accept the result; their impact is pervasive, implacable and destined to cause a reaction. That time of reckoning, the need to prove a separate identity, ripens into something steadfast during adolescence. Choosing friends represents that free will, an initial step beyond, bringing new and unusual to the table and announcing it as if a different person is in charge. In my life at least, "best friends" began a dynamic that had repercussions and led somewhere. As a twosome, we became something greater than our sum apart: a duo, a team, an enterprise — Sacco and Vanzetti, Rogers and Hammerstein, a pair of Little Rascals.

Bookchin and I had our brief symbiosis, our year of unlikely team — punctuated by a brilliant run of comet across the sky — and now I marvel as I sift through remains. In a way, the miracle was that we ever became friends. I was more of a jock; he was New York Yippie stock. I was a Mid-Western Catholic; he was New York Jew. I drank and smoked pot; he did neither. I admired E.B. White; he, Abbie Hoffman. I hung out with brawny no-minds; he with theater types and gay sophisticates. I studied, read and loved to write; he preferred "dabbling" in visual mediums like film and photography. His parents were counter-culture, living apart in open relationship; mine, well, you get the idea. There wasn't much in common; in a sense, it was about each of us being "uncommon".

Chez Bookchin was a counter-cultural throw-back: disheveled, unkempt, improvisational. Every time I went there, from the glow-in-the-dark solar system on his bedroom ceiling to a fancy 18-speed bike and the parade of Big Apple radicals passing through, I understood we occupied different realms. Joey frequently went to New York City on weekends, came home talking about exhibits, Broadway, concerts in the Park. Our senior year, he dated a 31-year-old documentary filmmaker in Manhattan, his dream relationship and career. He *was* Woody Allen, though young, assertive and without angst or self-doubt: he was "in-the-know", surrounded by personalities, culture, art, and riding the cusp of the cutting edge.

One of his dependable qualities was an instinct for playing the system. To this day, I am not sure how Bookchin got to college; or, I should say, I know how he got to college but am not sure how, or even if, he survived. He was a scattered, tangible kid; loved gadgets, could overcome anything verbally, lampooned with smart allusions but had no real appetite for study or book-learning. Tall, bent over, riddled with misspellings and cross outs, his left-handed script had a hard time staying on track and it took him forever to spit it out. I allowed him to look at test papers over my shoulder in Chemistry. In History, as I filled a blue-book and plowed into another, I left them under my seat where Bookchin would feign dropping something and come up with mine gaining some sense of what he needed with his own. We mickey-moused our way, or at least he did, impressing everyone with maturity and sophistication while skillfully covering the scholarly gaps.

On our first day as seniors, we pulled up in our car pool to an uncertain situation: the teachers were on strike and the school district was attempting to break the union by hiring replacements — the lunch ladies. (Yes, the lunch ladies.) We walked out front in a kind of daze. "Could this really be happening?" Rumors swept the hallway, and students milled uncertainly as classes were cancelled. It slowly dawned that this unrehearsed social vacuum was just our kind of opportunity. Mr. Meyers, Mr. Burns, Mr. Donoghue, Ms. Ayers, Ms. White, Mr. Dresser, even Mrs. Kerr were out on North Avenue walking the picket-line. The students, at least the mindless majority, seemed blasé about it: cheering the extension of vacation, apathetic about the prospect of substitutes. "Who cares who teaches us?" They averred.

Bookchin and I convinced each other that we needed to do something. We couldn't just talk about social change, then sit back and watch a union get busted; not to mention spending a month, a week or even a day with teachers who had no clue. The replacements were set to begin in the morning and we needed something big, really big, to keep kids from going to school. As far as I could tell, my fingers to the student body's pulse, there was one thing that would work: a keg party at North Park. Bookchin looked at me quizzically, his angular face, tight curls and knowing eyes showing that he was mulling it over. He brightened some, hunching in, giving that ironic look, "It might be just crazy enough to work."

We didn't worry about it being a school day, or that we weren't old enough to drink, or that we didn't have beer or permits or advance publicity. We decided right then and there to begin spreading the word. I found the right kids and told them flat: two kegs in the morning instead of school. Tell everyone, jocks, heads, townies, creeps, burn-outs and the fags. Reaction was favorable, a small brush fire was kindled, though student councilors were a little dismayed. They supported a boycott of classes all-right, but not civil, and especially uncivil, disobedience. We agreed to differ, then vaguely arranged to meet the next day at 2:00 on North Avenue.

Bookchin and I retreated to his place and began preparations. It was a small chore — we'd never had a kegger before — and we set about calling liquor stores, inquiring about prices, deposits, taps, cups. This seemed as natural to us as working on any school project, as if we had been in training for it all along — our teachers the faithful mentors and chief beneficiaries. Bookchin relished the revolutionary nature of our conspiracy: fomenting a real-life uprising. I was infatuated with the justness and disarming symmetry in our cause: kids getting to skip school, have a party, abandon apathy and help a union by sticking it to the callous administration.

We purchased the kegs that night — we had fake I.D.'s that Bookchin got mail-order — struggling to get them in garbage bags, wrap them in ice, lift them into the back of the Valiant. Despite being tall, Joey was no athlete, slender and almost effete; it was all we could do to heft them aboard. We leaned against the trunk after, puzzling over the tap, musing about who might come, projecting how it would go. We weren't nervous, but it was a kind of moment-of-truth: an actual improvisation as opposed to the theoretical stuff we fantasized about. I remember that Joey burst out gleeful at one point: "It's like we have two bombs in there ticking away, ready to explode." Neither do anarchist apples drop far from the tree.

The car pool rolled up the avenue a little different that day: two kegs disguised as a pair of squat sophomores. We didn't turn in at school but continued to the park. I can't pretend my memory is untarnished — we tapped the kegs by 10:00 — so I surrender all hope of a sequenced narrative. But I do have images which survive: A hazy uncertainty lingering even as a grey morning lifts, more and more kids showing up, some not yet 15. Joey screaming my name out and doing contortions to wrap himself around the keg as a ruffian fondles the tap; he had a credibility gap with townies who did most of the partying. The petition papers of 80-some names which I required everyone to sign before they got their glass and which I have kept faithfully all these years. Frisbees flying, the park littered with teenagers toting beer cups, joints popping up, but never cops or parents or city workers. The magic moment when the second keg slurped out and Joey and I raced to the Valiant, covering them in blankets. Walking out to North Avenue with a small group of revelers to meet another dozen or so students who had prepared signs with the help of the union. Marching down the avenue with a police escort rolling in front, emergency lights flashing. Joey's sister, a reporter for the alternative paper, exhorting us in a thick New York accent: "Joey, you hav' to get them chyaa-nting. Joey, listen to me. Chyant. Chyant like this —" Coming up the hill to the school with placards in both hands, yelling out: "No teachers, no school! No teachers, no school." The picket line suddenly coming into view, teachers running toward us, waving and embracing, some of them wiping at tears. Reaching the entrance where Bookchin and I ended up in a shouting match with the principle — our chants magnified by the sheltered overhang — as I wave beer-sotted petitions under his nose with signatures of every student who had skipped that day.

The whole episode succeeded beyond our wildest dream: We had a rollicking good time in the park, sold enough cups to break even, appeared that night on the television news and, in the morning, graced the front page of the *Burlington Free-Press* along with Principal Danyow. In two days the strike was settled, teachers were back at work, union solidarity was affirmed and Joey and I garnered respect from more disparate groups than thought possible. It was a blur, a blast — the bombs went off. I remember driving back from the liquor store that afternoon with the sun glints lowering but still brilliant over Lake Champlain. Joey was counting out money, dividing up our halves of the deposit. (He even paid in advance his pool dues for September.) We felt exhausted, emotionally drained but also alive to the biggest thrill of our lives. We had really done something, pulled off the big heist. Joey looked at me; I looked at Joey. We laughed, we hooted, we clasped hands triumphantly in front of the rear-view mirror. High school had never felt so fun, an unlikely friendship never this rich.

I still have the front-page photo from that day. Joey is looking on intently while another student has a hand to her forehead as if she can't believe what she hears. Both of my hands are full with petitions as I aggressively plead my case. Danyow looks uncompromising, not at all pleased. To tell the truth, I'm not even sure why I wanted to get involved that day; why I came to believe I had a role to play. I'm convinced that if it were just me alone I wouldn't have lifted a finger. But I had a friend. That was 25 years ago, and in some odd sense, even though I've lost everything else — all my relationships, that place, even specific knowledge of life back then — I have never been able to fully extricate myself from high school. It's where I determined to become someone, to redeem the loss of home and boyhood and find purpose in life. It may be a chimera, but I honestly believe that remnants of those who assisted in this passage are magically at work inside me right now, rooting me on, urging me to liberate as many as I can. And it's a process I renew every fall, every week, every morning as I pull open the heavy glass doors at school and duck inside.

into the looking glass

As much as individuals establish a modus operandi at a fairly young age, and as accurately as test designers pin-point success among adolescents, and as much as playing a musical instrument (I never have) or getting involved in extra-curriculars (basketball was it for me) are indicators of academic achievement, it would have been hard to forecast that the young man sitting in the back of Mrs. Kerr's French class in 1978, making faces and caustic remarks, was going to end up on three exchange programs, attend an elite college and read novels in French and Spanish, then become an energetic teacher of it all to youngsters within the next 10 years. I know that at a certain point *even I would have bet my life* against any of it happening. And perhaps, in a way, I did, and lost the whole damn wager — my life given over to teaching language — because that is exactly what happened.

Mrs. Kerr was a beast of a French teacher: large and disheveled, energetically challenged, pedagogically out to pasture. Her thin hair, dyed brown, usually worked itself up and out of position by the time we got to her room for 6th period. Arrayed unflatteringly in pants suits with a blouse — solid faded colors usually — she did not radiate much joy or pleasure in regards to Frenchiness. Narrow, small eyes plunged into the background of her corpulent face and it was not long before we buried them altogether with a circus of improvisations, devastating affronts to her authority and occasional half-hearted attempts to fill answers on worksheets. She hunched, glowering up front, trying in completely detectable ways, to convince us it was a serious class, that we needed French, that she really could pull this off. We laughed as students butchered phrases and she tried haplessly to get us back on track. French? *Foût le camp.*

In truth, what really mattered to this tossed salad of youngsters was to get through last period with genuine fun: chase Mrs. Kerr's goat until we had her cornered by cat-calls and general pandemonium, face red, arms thrown up — most of us dimly aware we were being quite cruel, even by our diminished adolescent standards. Needless to say, the year wrecked without a real language breakthrough, though I did acquire "savoir faire" in classroom disruption: a medicating balm for those who lacked attention growing up.

* * *

From this distance, it seems remarkable that I was even in French class. What business was it of mine to believe that French was part of my destiny or future? *Francais? Etes-vous serieux?* Not that I was totally without culture or sensibility. We were, after all, still rafting out the 60s turmoil and its attendant desire for openness and worldwide change. In 1972, when I was 12, my family ventured to Tucson for a month where both of my parents taught courses for St. John's University. We stayed in a convent dormitory, eating meals in their cafeteria near the center of town (if that's not an oxymoron in Tucson's case). One weekend, we drove to Nogales, Mexico in our Pontiac station wagon. I spent the trip down way in the back with my nose in a *Learn Spanish the Easy Way* book, looking at pictures, correlating vowel and pronunciations — *el libro, mi amigo, manzana* — hoping to put them to some indefinable use at the border.

Nogales was a mob scene: hearing street vendors and aggressive merchants pestering in broken English did little for my desire or ability with Spanish. *They* seemed to come to *us* more; on *our* terms and in *our* language. As always, my father insisted on trying his Spanish, cobbled together from an early study of Latin and military contact with Italians during the war — *No me gusta, compadre. Qué vale éste?* He had no intention of buying anything, but it charmed Mexicans holding blankets and jewelry and also contributed to his aura as father and college professor with his respective publics. But I left untransformed: language learning was tough business, if not impossible, to do alone. Neither my classes nor teachers provided any hope that success was in the cards.

Funny too, and how remarkable, to consider the next time I got to Nogales, 10 years later. It was 1981, mid-December, and I was a college student en route to a college program in Morelia, Mexico. I carried two trimesters of Spanish and a couple of exchanges abroad with a good grasp of French, a romance language stone's throw from *espagnol*. Still, I had never conversed with a native speaker before crashing the border where the Greyhound left me, having come overland from Minneapolis hitchhiking and arranging travel off university ride-boards. (I had some doozies.) My immediate goal was to get to the train station and head down the coast — San Blas or Puerta Vallarta were possibilities. I traveled in typical American fashion, a blue Kelty pack that served me well in Europe held clothes, books, food and toiletries.

Just across the border were money-changers, blanket vendors and a sea of hangers-on. Same old Nogales. I cashed traveler's checks and, after consulting *Let's Go Mexico!*, headed to where I thought a bus should pass. I asked a couple of Mexicans if this was the case. They confirmed — I believe — that it was. Still, apprehension mounted as I watched morning unfold amidst the whirling chaos of a border-town: roaring trucks, scurrying pedestrians, exotic cargo bikes. The sun warmed me to a new day — smells of frying food, putrid litter and exhaust combining in an indescribable way. And I felt suddenly alone; alone without a common language this time. Why did I do these things?

A girl steps forward and motions to me. "*Allá.*" She indicates — there is your bus. All I see is an oversized ice-cream van, like ones that played music in our neighborhood selling ice-pops out the back. It stops. People get off and on. I lift my pack up the steps and it lightens suddenly, then levitates above the crowd. They pass it, as of routine, over their heads onto a kind of luggage rack along the side of the…should I call this a bus? The back row is elevated into a bank of seats. There are metal benches along the sides, though most everyone is standing like me, crammed tight, clutching the overhead bar. I am next to the driver and a multitude of eyes are watching with bemusement, but I don't want to move because from here I can just manage a view forward while monitoring the safety of my gear.

The driver's shirt is open to the waist and a series of chains, pendants and necklaces dangle down. I can see through the gear box to pavement; an opening large enough to eat a child but obviously just routine. A fabric fringe frames the windshield, jiggling, swaying, and religious provisos ring out hailing Mary, asking for the love of Jesus. The radio blares a Mexican pop station, accordion-based rhythms with horns and bass, as we negotiate traffic, slowly leaving the dense part of the city, gaining the edge of town. This was nothing like Greyhound, still further from anything I knew in America, but I recognized its quality of genius and happenstance: a cultural charisma under hot sun I would come to value and appreciate.

My initiation to Mexico was not yet complete, however, not even with the driver stopping, pointing to the station and helping me down with my pack. Before I could board the train, I needed to get my Tourist Card stamped. There, in a sterile room off the main hall with chairs and a desk, an official went over my documents. He spoke accented English, though I tried my best in Spanish. "So, you are going to Morelia, to…study Spanish?" I nodded. "Well, in that case, you should not have a tourist visa, but a student visa." I frowned, telling him that school officials had never mentioned it. My visit would be less than 120 days, clearly allowed with the Tourist Card. He continued, informing me of regulations, how sure this all was, how he knew as a certified government official — though one without a uniform or credentials. "I tell you. We close to Christmas, no? For you, I give a present. I approve tourist visa." Smiling, he opens the drawer, pulls out a roller-pad and stamps my papers in three places. "There. Done, *bien hecho* and *Feliz Navidad.*"

I make as if to leave, but he presses the papers down. "I give *you* Christmas present, huh?... Now your turn; you give *me* present." I looked confused but straightened up quick. *La mordida,* the bite. I had read about it in materials our Carleton professor gave us. Later, in Morelia, I would see two traffic cops on a motorcycle, the one in the rear sitting backwards holding a stack of license plates, a screwdriver in his hand. Parking enforcement. In Mexico City, the motorcycle patrol eventually got so proficient that they took bribes out the window of cars they intended to stop: an impressive efficiency. Call it a cultural difference. There is always a way to rectify a legal problem or a procedural difference in Mexico, as long as you have *la plata, bakshish-dolares.* I pull out my wallet, leaf through and put a fifty down. "What? *Cincuenta pesos. Es insulto!* It does not buy even breakfast. "*Ni un desayuno!*" I was new to bribing, too.

"*Soy estudiante. Soy pobre.*" I throw down two more bills. He shot eyebrows to the ceiling, and in a gesture so practiced as to be automatic, drew the top-drawer, revealing an assortment of currency, swept the bills inside before closing promptly — brushing me on in the same motion. My initiation was done. Now I was free to go. Free to wait for hours for a late train. Free to freeze nearly to death over the long night of cold. Free to watch an incredibly picturesque Mexican countryside and rich, colorful life of its people unfold before me over the course of days.

We like to think that the U.S. is a nation of humble beginnings and common folk. But riding the coast train over four days into Mexico City helps one to realize the true depth of what that means. They too consider themselves *americanos*: wayfarers in a place infinitely large and diverse, overflowing with the humble and destitute, hopeful and hopeless, workers, travelers and seekers after a dream. I watch a multitude of families lurking and curious outside rickety shacks or gathered around flaming barrels as we chug by. In my imagination, this is 19th century immigrant America. It is confirmed as I go up and down the cars, lower class ones full of small stock, agricultural bundles, the smell of excrement. Old men, tired and stooped lean against the wall, straw hats folded onto their chests. Children are wrapped tightly to the backs of their mother. Eyes peek out brown and more brown above ponchos or beneath caps, content to have a spot, even on the cold and dirty floor of this passage to the next town, *la próxima*, another crossing over into the unknown.

Salmon Rushdie, an unfortunate expert in matters cross-cultural, has talked about borders in his book *Step Across This Line*. How odd are these walls that are holding back indefinitely the dissolution of human-made differences we call culture. They may be the last of our frontiers, and also from this perspective, the most valuable. In that defining line between here and there, a world is broken up into "visible and invisible, physical and metaphorical, amoral and moral." As Rushdie has said, it is a kind of "wake-up call" for the person looking to cross. I heard and felt this instinctively. It was like I traded in one self at that moment of crossing over and got handed a completely new identity. One without a recognizable past or stories, completely dependent on what I could make happen in the present. And I had to do it with someone else's tongue, which in reality, *por lo mejor o peor*, was my tongue as well.

This crossing over felt like a worthwhile adventure, an odyssey that mirrored other journeys for me growing up: always pushing into new territory, "me" as an unfolding experiment, a chronic explorer re-discovering himself in new states and towns and neighborhoods. Transformation can get to be a habit, a necessity, even an addiction, with the desire to constantly move on becoming the sole unifying element of a person's character. Perhaps this is more true of Americans than other people. In such cases, it is both an escape and a transgression and one not to be undertaken too lightly.

In Mexico, I put my time in. In the sky I recognized clouds from my boyhood when I wondered if afternoon baseball games would be rained out. But everywhere else, in the fields, flowers, insects, birds, and animals, I sensed exotic difference. Every small Mexican town and fleeting encounter reminded me that the presiding deities were wholly different than anything I was familiar with. And even at that I was nowhere close to cracking the code: social norms, gender expectations, religious compulsions, the entire gamut you learn only by being from a place. There was a wide way to the world, and no space for me to hide, to pretend I wasn't unusual, new, exceptional. The intensity of crossing that line changed everything around and about me.

* * *

The journey we undertake is filled with contingencies, unknowables. We cross boundaries and borders regularly, even when unaware. There is not a "standard" way of growing up; nor should there be. No one could have predicted my interests and sparse talent would coalesce around language or travel. I was not a particularly gifted nor enthusiastic language-learner; by the time I got to Mrs. Kerr, I was considerably less than that. The reason I drifted into French is that my sister Rebecca had blazed a trail, discovering an energetic, knowledgeable teacher in South Bend — Mrs. Bowler. I had her in 7th grade: small and perky, prim and proper — she was *trés francaise*, with a cooing, chirpy manner, nattering on whether we understood her or not. I followed Rebecca in Burlington, too, taking up French with the intention of joining Total Immersion, a full-fledged exchange program with Bergerac, a provincial town in southern France. (*Oui, Cyrano* country.)

The program took students out of school for an entire semester, putting us in a group member's home where we worked with a teacher who eventually went with us to France. In this case, it meant Olga, the unusual directress. She had a last name, but it was Russian and everyone just called her Olga: kind of foreboding, especially as you got to know her. She had lengthy blondish hair, graying over, thick wire-rim glasses and tended to dress in long, dark skirts and layered woolens, much like the eastern European she was. Plain, deeply pored, her brusque no-nonsense manner made her somewhat cold. Combined with an unfortunate protruding mole on her forehead, it pretty much clinched her reputation with us as a witch. She had been around the block, though, a true world traveler capable of disarming the *boulanger* as easily as the *conciérge*, *chauffeur, serveur, marchand, etcetera*.

Getting out of school daily, going to a nice home and learning French as a prelude to flying to Paris was an ideal scenario. The only real hurdle here was Olga, since school now meant five long hours a day under her thumb — lecturing us about literature, history, philosophy and art. She had practical units too, on "*politesse*," table manners, French customs, toileting, shopping, the metric system. Her repertoire was complete with the inhaling, aspirated "*oui*" which we figured was her own little tick, but which we soon realized was a demonstration of how incredibly European she was. The hour between 1:30 and 2:30 dragged like a glacial epoch, each minute scraped painfully across our consciousness and pressed irredeemably into our minds as one more episode of Olga going on about France.

But it all led to the magic day's arrival. We assembled like undisciplined rabble at the airport in Montreal and filed excitedly onto a 747 for our overnight flight to Paris. Bookchin was there, an assortment of others, and of course, Olga shepherding us at every juncture. This unfolded before me almost like a supernatural experience. There we were, arrayed across rows, listening to music on head phones or tuning in a movie; most of us too buzzed to do anything but gab, eyes on fire and attentive — *les jeunes américains en route à Paris*. When we broke beneath clouds over Paris, I had the sensation of being in another world, on another planet. Each little detail, every aspect of culture, from dress to cars to houses, struck me as unique, fascinating. I rode up front in the small Citroen cargo truck sent to get us. My eyes filled with wonder as Paris loomed up then swallowed us in a sea of unusual vehicles, billboards, traffic circles and internationalist architecture. Once on the ground, exuberance rolled on undiminished: elegant, unapproachable women, newsstands, the *tobaccanistes, le boucher,* the baker, the candlestick maker — all of it so incredibly French.

In a psychic sense, what I experienced was the complete redrawing of my paradigm of experience: some Jungian synchronicity and Joycian epiphany combined that forever affected the way I see the world. I believe it was connected to being young, to suddenly being released from the domain of gravity that I took as overriding and throwing myself head-long into every new experience. It went on like this for much of the three weeks I stayed in France: biking along rolling hills, executing social exchanges, appreciating the echoes and voices residing in a French family. And, of course, the language grew on me too, steadily, stealthily as I read, asked directions and ordered in restaurants. That gibberish I ignored and spoofed only a year before was gaining, revealing itself as the core lens through which one sees and responds to experience.

On the train from Paris to Bergerac, I arrived armed to the hilt with French wine. I had learned how to shop. About six of us staged a romp in our compartment, drinking right from the bottle, eating an assortment of cheeses and chocolates spread out on baguettes. *Trés américain, n'est-ce pas?* Periodically, I got up, dropped the window, put my entire head outside and screamed at the passing countryside, a torrent of air distorting my cheeks. Trains go awfully fast in France and drinking without regular meals or a good night's sleep is not a prescription for a great *ésprit de corps.* Shortly after I met my family in the tiny hamlet of *Le Fleix,* I came down with a wicked fever and sore throat. It must have been Strep. They were very considerate, the cement-man father, cleaning-woman mom, and drove me to a rural French doctor. She was considerate, too, a little formal, but willing to write a prescription before we headed out to the small village *chez les grand-parents* where we would be spending the weekend. What a bad break getting sick like this, I thought — ostensibly unaware how my own excesses had brought it on.

I layed in bed in some distant town delirious, almost completely unable to swallow because of the inferno raging in my throat. The women in the house worried and made certain one of their men got the prescription filled right away. Coming to and from my room, I could hear their heels click and echo as I drifted in and out of sleep. My temperature was still going up — *encore plus haut*! I remember them waking me in wan light, their faces concerned. They had a pill in their hand; I struggled to sit up. They demurred, withdrawing, starting an explanation. In my grogginess and lack of French — my visit was less than a week old — I didn't really follow until they got to: "*Il ne faut pas avaler. C'est une suppositoire.*" I pieced together the "don't swallow" part, but I had never heard of a suppository. What was that? And more importantly, what did I do with it if I couldn't swallow it?

I looked at one woman; she was out of French, but made a kind of gesture, pushing the pill upward as it rested on her finger-tip. It looked like a bullet. 'Oh my God!' I thought to myself. 'You have got to be joking.' "*Il ne faut pas avaler. C'est une suppositoire.*" She gestured again. *O.K., O.K., je comprends.* In the darkness I did something I had never considered before and might well go the rest of life without doing again, surprised, if somewhat embarassed, at being able to do it with such facility. *Initiation francaise*!

The next day, I felt much better. (Suppositories do work quickly.) I watched the men butcher a couple of chickens out back, catching blood in a vessel so that a special dish could be made. It was a little gruesome but anthropologically a gold mine. The women cooked all morning, windows steamed, and by noon had a feast beyond anything I had ever seen. We sat around an enormous U-shaped series of tables, set with china and regal linens, eating course after course, drinking wine, ("*Non, mérci.*") passing serving bowls, talking endlessly in the emotional way French families do. Later, I walked through the village which was engulfed in festival, old men in berets playing *boule*, young children trying their luck at shooting galleries, smells of fried dough and sugar — I was back in the hunt, thrilled as ever to be somewhere beyond my knowing, not at all looking forward to going home.

* * *

I loved my years of language learning and travel, but had absolutely no interest in becoming a teacher. The path I journeyed into education was late in forming and somewhat improvised. Yet, I consider myself lucky to have entered through the door of language instruction. It taught me two valuable things about classroom instruction — intimately related: One, students need to enjoy being in class, to have genuine fun with what they are asked to do. Two, they need to work on authentic tasks, ones that emerge from real life or bear upon their real life, to get so engrossed that skill development happens at an almost unconscious level. This kind of learning, intrinsic and self-directed, capitalizes on natural curiosity and enthusiasm. It propels a student forward acquiring all manner of skills without repair to formal study or regimentation, tapping an essential instinct to learn.

This became plain to me for good reason: I had essentially failed at learning Spanish as a boy alone with a book; failed at French in the class-room of Mrs. Kerr; failed even with Olga in Total Immersion — my French capacity growing very slowly compared to the hours expended. It was only being in France, curious to see more, asking directions, deci-phering crucial meanings, that propelled me forward. Having miserably failed more than once provided a vivid contrast for me about what worked.

I realized this only after trying to teach unsuccessfully — failing yet again — in ways that I had been taught by my high school teachers, as if being a younger Mrs. Kerr or a friendlier Olga (without an alarming birth-mark) was all I could imagine. As genuine as my intention might have been, I know now that there is no substitute for skillful, well-designed lessons and pedagogy. As Marshall MacLuhan, the media critic, might have said had he been an education professor: "The methods are the message." True, personal integrity and character are more crucial, but you probably don't have much of either if you haven't bothered to learn the best methods in a particular field. The biggest misconception I had as a young educator was believing that being "nice" alone would allow me to succeed as an instructor: I only wanted to be liked, believing that if I was "friendly," student learning would take care of itself.

Watching an experienced and talented teacher, like a Spanish instruc-tor I observed in St. Paul before I was licensed, Mr. Millen, confirmed how wrong I was. This guy had a total mastery of the classroom, making sounds or faces for each student as he took attendance, playing row against row in competitive games, drilling vocabulary on the fly, using mime, visuals, and realia as he went, never once leaning on English. Total energy and absorption in the moment. Students had a great time, *all 43 of them* crammed into his room. The man had a honed technique, had perfected his system, understood how to work with and enjoy students as well as the larger community. He was "nice" and well-liked, principally because he was so committed to student learning and had such a complete repertoire of teaching techniques.

And taking workshops from similarly energetic instructors clued me in to what kinds of activities — fun ones — were appropriate for different levels of language instruction. I learned to play "20 Questions" or "I'm thinking of a thing..." as ice-breakers, to spice up classes with games and competitions, to create rewards for language use, to frame projects around real-life needs and tasks. Especially, I learned how to be goofy and glad myself; a kind of language clown alert to using French or Spanish as a way of poking fun, teasing, suggesting what an endless spoof is this time we have together. I called kids with disconnected phones, put on disguises, tossed out berets, performed one-man shows, juggled, led them in calisthenics — adding each of these over time.

A small light bulb lit up inside me. I grasped intuitively that teaching language authentically, completing genuine tasks — not just demanding right answers — was clearly the way to proceed. And more: that a teacher must find their own circuitous, riotous, untidy path to get through to the kids. There were not formulas or a standard script for making it work. As with being a student or having to learn anything, the journey to becoming a teacher is one of individual discovery, driven by a personal sense of responsibility. And I should know. I had gone from dead in the water (*un zéroe*) as a French student, and even as a haphazard teacher, to reasonably competent and *enthusiastique* in a short period.

* * *

My first instructional experiences informed me that I was only so-so as a French and Spanish teacher and this served as motivation to improve, learn more, which I did over time. But it also reminded me that language instruction was not the reason I went into teaching: it was, in fact, a kind of add-on, a way to ensure I got hired. Writing and literature were my first loves. The teaching market was tight in the late '80s. One way to guarantee an interview and a contract was to offer "flexibility." I had three fields: English, French, Spanish, plus basketball coaching. It was the kind of versatility that administrators worship because of shifting enrollments and the challenge of finding staff in specialized areas. I got a fairly quick offer from a private Minneapolis high school, De La Salle; ironically for me, a long-time Catholic stalwart near downtown on an island in the Mississippi.

For four years there, I hammered away at becoming a language teacher, handling French courses, picking up what was left of the Spanish program from the deeply despised lady down the hall. (Mrs. Kerr — with spit balls and dampened paper wads thrown in.) I was not immediately successful, though my courses improved as I learned to balance fun with the requirements of learning. In some ways, it was an ideal place to find instructional legs, consolidate skills, but it was not home, if ever I am destined to find one. For one thing, the pay was hideous. I rode bike to work because I couldn't afford to drive. Another thing was the Catholicism. It brought up the whole uncomfortable issue from my past. I was expected to lead prayers before every class and did so in a vague way, using French or Spanish, invoking peace, *humanismo* or *amour*, delivering it so that only occasionally did students inquire as to what I had just said. It was more play than piety for me, but the kids were inculcated into a system to which I did not subscribe, nor wish to perpetuate. I was recovering from being a Catholic myself. I felt ambivalent, not only toward the school's outward message, but my own inward disavowal of it.

More daunting was the lack of professionalism and resources. When Bob Dole ran for President in 1996, he toured De La Salle, extolling it as a model for all that is right about "school choice" in America. To be fair, De La Salle had a handful of excellent teachers, a great basketball program, storied alumni and a long tradition in Minneapolis. But realistically, how many extra public school students could fit in their antiquated building? Fifty, 75? And whose choice would it really be to go there? The students? There was only one counselor for nearly 400 kids, no special education teachers, no nurse, no special services and no social worker. Supplies, uniforms, transportation, even lunches were substandard. Students were in charge of washing boards, sweeping floors and emptying trash, though if you wanted it done, it was best to stick around or simply do it yourself. Teachers were responsible for completing their own copying on the antiquated copy machine and numbers were closely monitored. Religious personnel were dragged to the school from far-off posts and expected to exact spiritual renewal at the point of teaching in the inner city. Morale was moribund, many teachers going through the motions, meekly following directives from above, I suppose in their mind, for the good of the Church.

An incident from my first year stands out to me as typifying my experience in an under-funded Catholic school. I taught Spanish in the afternoon and was working with subject pronouns — he, she, we, you — introductory material. I felt good about my approach, pointing to a person or group, asking for the appropriate pronoun. I point to Marquise, the class says "*él*"; I point to Angela and Sarah, "*ellas*"; I point to a group of boys, "*ellos*"; I point to Samantha, the class says "*él*," and then laughs uproariously. I pause, "*No clase.*" I point again to Samantha, they say "*él*" again, more laughter. I correct this time — "*Ella*" I say. "*Clase, repitan, por favor, ella.*" I listen: half say "*ella*," but another half definitely say "*él*." I get an intuition that something is wrong and that more drilling is not going to straighten it out. Samantha is a chunky kid with short hair and acne around her cheeks. I have to admit she definitely looks like a guy and dresses like one too, in baggy jeans and untucked flannel shirts. I also remember how she came to me on the first day requesting that I call her "Sam" which is how she was known around school.

I switch gears to the next activity, bring the class home to the bell, remind them to do their homework, but I am not happy. I walk directly to the office and corner the one counselor, a pleasant guy, short with a beard and penetrating eyes. "Is there something I should know about Samantha Williams?" He takes a breath, pulls me aside, explaining that she is a special case, wants to be treated as a boy, is in a program for gender issues and will probably seek an operation when she/he turns 18. That "ahah" feeling rises within me, followed closely by, "Well, don't you think you should tell her...his... teachers about this?" He nods vaguely. "Kind of busy just now. That's a good suggestion. Maybe I can get out a memo."

Professionals who are overworked, under-trained or not well compensated lead inevitably to one thing: children being left to chance. De La Salle is willing to throw you into that breach, as are most schools, hoping that you somehow bridge the gap, meet those needs. If you can't, they'll understand. The bell will ring in any case, marking day's end. At that point all of us go home: ones who are secure, happy and comfortable as well as ones who aren't. We'll come back and give it another shot. Some will try harder than others. It seems a little half-hearted, mechanical even, but it's the way we typically do it. We put our time in, and though needs of students continue to grow and magnify, our efforts remain constant. There is no special reward, commendation or bonus pay if you stay late with a kid or put extra time toward a lesson. All things are not equal: not between schools, not amongst teachers, and certainly not when it comes to students. The human element seems strangely divorced from education's status as just a job.

After four years, I decided to move from De La Salle for one very important reason: they were unable to shift me into teaching English, despite consistent and persuasive appeals. And God must indeed work in mysterious ways, because if they had, I might be there now unclogging a urinal or convincing someone that *Dead Poet's Society* is not an incitement to suicide. The more I taught French and Spanish, the more convinced I became I was not like most language teachers: not like an arch Francophile, nor a determined *maéstro* of all things Spanish. I did not create culturally appropriate bulletin boards, celebrate holidays in song, nor have days where every student brought ethnic food. I just didn't care much about these and instead hoped to equip students with a love of language, a sense of play, the desire to get over there soon. Teaching language was never my deep mission, my "raison d'être," however rich my individual experience.

At the end of May in 1992, I sat up front in my 1940s padded-leather chair as students worked on exams. I knew this would be my last class, the last time I would work with them. They had learned to enjoy my courses — some of them for four years — to enjoy me personally, even looking up to me as someone positive in their educational life. My personal style of instruction had fused with the subject matter just as surely as Olga's methodology had defined everything French in my adolescent mind.

If anything, these determined, decent kids were the best part of being at "De." How could you not love them? Their lively personalities were the one thing that brightened my day in that back hallway of an imposing institution that echoed incessantly wherever you walked. The same place that had once enshrined corporal punishment as routine policy and for most of its history had admitted only young men was where I learned the joys of being with youngsters again: girl, boy, white, black, Native, Asian, gay, Agnostic, and pierced. I cried. Tears leaked down as I turned away. No one noticed, not even Josh, who came to ask — in French — if he could use *le pissoir.* I aspirated my *"oui,"* looking down as if grading, though a splash hit the page. I rubbed it off; this old twinge of pain embarrassed me. It was about the relationships I would be missing; tender bonds that I would have to, once again, rupture as I moved on somewhere else.

* * *

I was happy to discover the next fall that a large public school like Park Center, on the inner ring of suburbs around Minneapolis, did a more effective job with young people overall than De La Salle. For one, morale was higher. Teachers and staff actually laughed and enjoyed themselves at meetings or chatting in rooms after school. There were a multitude of resources to help teachers with nettlesome student conflicts — counselors, a social worker, administrators, even a fully staffed Special Education Department as mandated by federal law. There were "paras," departmental secretaries who handled typing, ordering and copying tasks, and custodians who cleaned the building and handled small repairs. Departmental offices were equipped with books, supplies, telephones, even a computer. Sure, once the bell rang you were still on your own, but between classes, before and after school, if you had issues, there were a multitude of professionals ready to lend an ear or a hand. Staffings on particular students involving parents and all their teachers were not uncommon. The atmosphere for learning was generally brighter, more open. And students, at least it seemed to me, were friendlier, not so resistant to authority or heavy expectations of the institution as a whole.

This does not mean everything was roses. Park Center was almost four times the size of tiny De La Salle; while both schools had a healthy degree of diversity, it lacked that feeling of being a tight-knit community. These kids came from all over the racial and economic spectrum and trying to infuse a common spirit involved an alchemy beyond the administration's ability. You only ever knew so many kids in the hallway; it took me several years just to get the names of regular staff members. There was a vibe that things could — possibly — get out of hand. Fights, threats, drugs and weapons were more common, though I rarely saw any. So was truancy and the potential among kids for total rejection of learning as a means to a better future. Here was a true cross-section of America's child output, not a self-selected sample of parents who just wanted their kids out of public school.

I took the change as an opportunity, for the first time drawing a decent salary, treated like a professional educator. My heart went out to every unmotivated, recalcitrant, unfocused kid in the building, imagining that he or she could have been me in an earlier incarnation. I identified with their being lost, having no idea what they wanted, yet possessing enough intellectual fuel that the right spark might light up their whole being. Unfortunately, it was also stressful and disappointing to find myself in a department that had such a practiced indifference toward these same kids.

I came to realize that a number of teachers had no interest or ability in getting beyond the way they were taught in school, dismissing whole groups of youngsters as incapable of learning. At the time, it felt like I had made a new insight: ineffective teaching wasn't limited to a tired Catholic institution; it was endemic to the trade.

To make a long story short, my creative methods and zany teaching style got to be an issue because students were shuttled back and forth between teachers every trimester. It meant that we were supposed to stay together, literally on the same page, yoked like clumsy oxen, teaching identical material — drilling and killing, handing out the same exams, looking for the same useless answers. Many students wanted to stick with my classes and teaching style; unflattering comparisons were made, sometimes involving parents, which then got back to staff. The administrator in charge was bright enough to understand and confront the issue openly, trying to use me as a wedge to breathe fresh air into a department gone stale, but at the end of the day he too surrendered to the reality of being stuck with a tenured gang of traditionalists. The school's language instruction was not about to change because a maverick was on the scene. But, neither was I about to change to fit a mediocre program. I lost a battle for pedagogical innovation but won an ally in a very key position and by spring, the administrator was feeding me a steady but increasing diet of English courses.

* * *

One of the places I ended up was team-teaching World Literature and World Area Studies with a colleague from Social Studies. It gave me stability at a time I was inured to change, allowing me to work on relationships over an entire year in a building where having the same group for more than a trimester was rare. And it gave me leave to burrow deeply into ideas, creating well-considered units while spiraling specific skills around the books and materials we used.

Getting to the core values of Africa's prolific cultures, examining closely China's wisdom traditions, picking apart the influences in Western Civilization has sharpened my focus as a teacher and reshaped how I consider the world. I doubt I could have been so open to these truths if I hadn't developed a respect for other cultures by living in them and seeing firsthand that America's experience is only one thread — and a very recent one — in an ancient tapestry. It feels exactly like how I start my World Literature course each year: asking students to imagine a journey around the world, across time, encountering cultures very different, yet oddly resonant, to their own. I ask that they bring an open mind, an ample heart and a commitment to engage unique places and issues. I also tell them if they remain alert, they will come back having learned more about themselves and their own culture than anything else.

That's how it happened as a young man when I traveled to France in high school, then France and Mexico again in college. You put yourself out there to discover another culture and end up staring furtively in the mirror realizing, perhaps for the first time, what makes you unique. The yardstick by which you measure yourself and your country expands into three dimensions: deepens in appreciation for qualities taken for granted, heightens in criticism of things short-sighted or provincial, deflects for matters which are trivial or routine. It's not something you can plan for or realize without adventure, without leaving home and caution behind, abandoning yourself to the experience of full discovery. And it's an experience that happens too rare amongst Americans today, caught as we are in the rush to advance at home, enamored of comforts we take as of right and which only living abroad, particularly in the developing world, places in perspective.

I realize that I have been hard on language instructors because of their unimaginative, outdated pedagogy. Yet there is something terribly important about their effort on behalf of languages and cultures. The United States has a generally dreadful reputation with the world: of being out-of-step with an ethic that seeks to harmonize and build relationships across borders. We are too often viewed as arrogant, self-absorbed, uninterested in connecting with distant places, as being mired in prejudice and ethnocentrism. And we shouldn't be. Power and might alone will not win us friendship and respect; wealth and technology are not the only things the rest of the world values in an encounter with us. The Mrs. Bowlers, Olgas, Mrs. Kerrs, and Mr. Millens all believe in the crucial importance of teaching that we are not alone: that an entirely different approach thrives out there. They exude hope for pushing back the frontier and dissolving the startling distance that a line creates between an "us" and a "them."

This is vital work, bespeaking a person of hope. One who realizes that in our continued connection, the human family is galvanized to the wondrous creation we represent as a whole. And especially — most crucially — that we are a whole, despite obvious and profound differences. This family of distant cousins and unknown relatives is meant to stand as one, to undo cheap prejudice, overcome misconceptions, dissolve stereotypes. We are intended to value each other's beauty and achievement, and through dedication to this principle in education, to speak each other's tongue.

Scratch a language professional almost anywhere and you will find a person who once stumbled onto the set of a foreign land and mastered a part they never imagined. They came to see themselves and their culture differently by learning the intricacies of a new place; a place without which they cannot now imagine being the same. By transgressing boundaries and undoing acculturation, they reversed the formula upon which this nation was founded and became, for a time, something other than another ignorant American.

you want to be a teacher?

I had a student several years ago, Peter. A tall kid, stiff but personable and creative, a barometer type. Prominent brow, eyes a little sunk, big lashes; Lurch-like in a way. He wasn't an athlete or musician, nor in the theater group. His grades were good but not exceptional. Other students found him interesting, perhaps strange, because you couldn't really pigeon-hole him, though he did a good job of making friends and keeping them. He wore modish clothes, second-hand stuff, thin shirts, corduroys, and in winter kept a scarf around his neck. Mostly, his strength was about being grounded, having lived in the area all his life, his mother a district employee. That made him stable and alert, above the crowd at keeping things in perspective. He had contacts across different high school groups — jocks, heads, brains, townies, freaks, even kids who denied being part of any group, which was everyone.

One of his buddies, John, was in class with him. John was charismatic, bright, likeable but highly erratic, irresponsible, even condescending. Still, they hung out. Somewhat plain in stature and appearance, John made up for it with his mouth, whispering cuts, tossing off cracks or questioning a possible contradiction as I lay out material. He was bright all right, a real intellectual firecracker whose whiz-bang intellect might fizzle as easily as go off in your face. He was from working class stock and had mutated into a kind of "rebel-brain," standing against high school as being inimical to personal freedom. Peter was just the person to see his strengths, keep him from blowing up or blowing off.

Late senior year, John got picked up with a small amount of speed and designer drugs and spent some time in county jail. Dealing, or hoping to. Peter took it to heart — he prided himself on having never smoked nor drank — stopping me in the hall, his throat lumped. I told him what I knew about knocks in life's cupboard, kicked some at the carpet, made sure he understood to find a future no matter what others did. That is, as seems to happen a lot, I didn't have good answers. He shuffled to college, eventually transferred to the university, went abroad and had a fun but academically routine career like a million others. Except that he never lost touch. Every year or so, a note, a letter or eventually an e-mail would appear detailing his doings, inquiring after life back at school.

Five years later he showed up. Tall, distinctive and beyond youth, we chatted about career choices: teaching or film school. It's not like I have a ton of energy after five classes, so I hunched understandably: "Be an artist or teach them." He thought it best to start an internship right away as requirements were 50 hours before any application to a degree program. John, it turned out, was a banker-mortgage officer type, made the dough, owned his own house; well on his way to six figures, a wife, kids and reasons to vote Republican. Pete was in touch with him, too.

That winter, Peter sat in back of class Fridays and sometimes paid close attention, though more likely just absorbed. He cancelled when busy or just didn't show, did homework, every once in a awhile after a morning would chip in: "You're the master, Hen." As his graduate application deadline loomed he wavered about becoming a teacher: "Will I like it? What about money? Is this the right thing? Do you have any advice?"

I rounded up the usual rationales: *It's good for your soul. Human contact keeps you vital. Imagine summers off.* "You'll be poor but learn a hell of a lot." Because of me or in spite of me, he delayed the university program, heading to Japan to teach English and give it some hands-on first. He recently wrote seeking last thoughts about pursuing a degree and included this, explaining his need to feel connected: "If someone wrote to me, 'It's still cold, the (sport teams of Minnesota) can't seem to hold their own in the playoffs, and 35W South is worse than ever,' that would be a great letter to me. It's good to know the state of things." Uh-huh. There's a certain appreciation for life's processes there. This desire for connectedness means he'll do fine as a teacher, as long as he lands an inspiring field. I'll tell him that next time he comes by.

* * *

"What if it turns out I can't teach?" is a common concern for someone thinking about teaching and a question I considered myself. In fact, it haunted me, or perhaps, drove me on. I had substantial evidence that as a front and center speaker, I was embarrassing. Or felt embarrassed — hot, red, tongue-tied — the only naked person in a room. This is not something I have put to sleep exactly, this fear of speaking; I manage to make a mess at times even now. It first manifested in high school at a political forum. I got handed a question by the family of Madeleine Kunin, first woman governor in the country. I stood up to a meager crowd, equal parts youth and adult, realizing that my heart pounded and sentences came as easily as stabbing mercury with a fork. I haven't the faintest what I asked about but got a strong feeling for the issue: Where did words go? What happened to the "me" who started to say something coherent?

Having to speak before a group, even just composing an introduction gave me tremendous anxiety. I convinced myself I couldn't do it, that I would end up stammering, spluttering. As I internalized this, I sometimes imagined I was not "real" as a person; that I was hiding something, was essentially a "faker": wrong, bad — perhaps even, evil. In my unsystematic way, I connected this to moving so much — Burlington was my sixth school in six years. Maybe I had developed a kind of inferiority from not having a home where I was known, understood; and, like most adolescents with a problem, felt self-conscious about it, set my internal dialogue up to a fevered pitch. Or perhaps, as I reason now, it was more about tripping over the basic truth of how this life works: you create yourself every moment. Continually. There is no way to avoid the crucible of public performance. Like sitting on the stool on a semi-regular basis: everyone has to do it.

Freshman year at Carleton, 1979. My roommate is Eric. We introduced each other to our dorm floor, maybe 30, 40 kids. Admittedly, I only knew him a few hours, but he was likely the most flamboyant freshman at school. Thin-boned and dark with a clipped British accent, he played guitar, wrote poetry, gave backrubs and communed over sprout sandwiches: California before it was cliché. Anyway, I panick, I sweat, my heart races as my turn gets close. There are a lot of suburban kids, white and friendly, tackling this "coming out" with good humor and equipoise. Eric goes, shining like a politician under lights, making me out to be Jimmy Dean, an admixture of E.B. White and dash of Voltaire. He, as Hawaiian shaman with access to past lives, knew these things. My turn: "This is Eric from California. He likes to play the guitar." That's all I could muster, face red, voice quaking. Dead, and I do mean "dead" silence ensued. What a sop I felt. After that, people looked at me like: "There's the poor shmuck that won't make it past freshman."

To great discomfort, there were times when my voice — whole body — was so shaky that I felt like dying, or at least shriveling from the spotlight. That Flintstone feeling where Fred shrinks under ridicule, "*wah-wah-wah-waaaahhhh*," until he's just a miniature, his voice a squeaky rasp. That was me. A tiny hard-hat in front of groups. Several times, in less formal situations, I split, going for air or locking myself in a bathroom and splashing cold water on my face. It didn't feel remotely funny. I had something serious to be self-conscious about. At its simplest, it was fear of public speaking, not highly unusual. (Surveys say that up to 90 percent of people fear public speaking.) At its most elaborate, my very being felt at risk, an imposter inside. Each time I went to a seminar or workshop I felt I risked everything; if an introduction came around that included my last meal.

Considering it now, I have an inchoate judgment that my father was involved; his imprimatur hangs around my neck in this as much as I mantle it for the sake of my success. Odd though, because he was an excellent speaker as a professor and a small-town politician — able to give presentations without notes, add-libbing as he went. He had shined at a young age, developed a winning formula — gaining election to the School Board and three times mayor of St. Cloud — and wanted the same for his children. In fact, with his black, square-framed glasses, he expected it, even at times demanded it, though I'm not sure I ever felt completely comfortable addressing him directly. His brooding presence in our home was a kind of local weather pattern. If quiet and calm, better for all of us to keep it that way. And what effects this has on a child — emotional detachment, strict command, considerable expectation — besides an exaggerated fear of approval and authority, I would need someone else to explain. Yet if I close my eyes and think about my fear of speaking, I imagine him there in the background, well-dressed and proper, waiting to disapprove.

After graduation from college I continued to flounder. In my first position at a small energy firm, my boss asked me to give a presentation at a conference. It was a tiny assignment, miniscule really — sharing results of pressurization tests in new home construction — but it mushroomed to unmanageability. I bargained to get out of it, flirted with calling in sick, spent days rehearsing what I would say to hundreds hunched over lunch plates. In the final terror-stricken moments, I was a mess: I forgot things, didn't eat, drifted in conversation. In a large hall of professionals I gave my little spiel quickly, mechanically. No problem. *De Nada.* As I finished, a hand shot up with a question I didn't quite understand and to which I could offer nothing but a flustered "Ah... ah... ah." My heart sank. A supervisor put the fire out as I sat down, ripening like a cherry. The question had been pretty basic: a technical term in regards to the type of pressure readings we used. (Science, never my bag.) More proof I was a social misanthrope, and did I mention it yet? Dumb. Very dumb.

I told myself that phobias like this felt more terrifying and debilitating inside than they appear. (And actually, as I well know, groups feel embarrassed for someone who is nervous to a remarkable degree — some quirk of empathy. Almost no one points and laughs.) It is the unnatural terror in the stomach which makes this unbearable, and like many self-imposed traumas seems entirely beyond relief or treatment. It eats at you, convinces that *you* are the actual issue here; you, who are such an embarrassment that how can you ever hope to get a handle on it? I sought outside assistance. A couple of bargain-basement therapists found me well-adjusted, even in good form comparatively, assuring me I would be okay, that such anxieties were common.

I also joined a 12-step group for Adult Children of Alcoholics: more because I shared characteristics of being from a dysfunctional family than needing to cope with any effects from my mother's late-life fling with wine. There in a room off the hall I tried to introduce myself to a dozen other first-timers, botching it so completely that all the facilitator did was offer a hug and encourage me, in the motto of the group to "Keep coming back." I did, soon volunteering to do a reading from the 12-step book. For a week, it was all I thought about, like that energy symposium all over again. Unusually pensive and preoccupied, I even slipped descending my back steps at home bruising my butt severely enough to walk with a limp.

Arriving early for the meeting, I discovered the door to the church basement locked. *Shit.* My nerves were churning my stomach; I needed a bathroom. I went in the back, walking like a stork, dropped my pants amidst some lilac bushes, pushing in my rear in as best I could. This is a bottom-barrel experience and like most bottoms, both hard and important to acknowledge. Here a man with a college education, a responsible job, a house and a hefty mortgage was reduced to skid row — bumming and slumming — all for the sake of reading out loud in front of 50 or 60 empathic souls in a church basement. I covered dutifully with leaves and grass and, straightening up, realized a couple of boys had discovered me. I limped out quick. Inside, I felt somewhat shaken as I closed my eyes, listening: "*Step 1: I admitted to myself and others that my life had become unmanageable.*"

That church basement became my home every Monday night; I kept going back for five years. It wasn't that I was a true believer in "the program"; my experience with Catholicism had me wary of falling for any spiritual agenda. Rather, I had simply followed my sister's example (Rebecca again) seeing how much she had grown in confidence, changed by being a part of the group. I referred to the process as "recovery", though from what, family, low self-esteem, Catholicism, has never been clear. Meeting consistently with others, learning from their courage — grappling with issues way beyond mine — felt therapeutic. It wasn't all of a sudden or fell instantly into place. I worked bit by bit, week by week, locating deep principles I could trust. Perceiving a power greater than myself loose in the world, I found ways to offset fear, certain, for the first time, that goodness and love wrapped themselves around the core of being human.

Out of these varied experiences, I decided to go into teaching. Despite what the rest of this manuscript might presage, it wasn't something I ever thought about or discussed. I watched the cohort I graduated from college with move into corporations or take up residence in graduate schools. Meanwhile, I held down a series of part-time jobs — tutoring, painting, clerking a used-book store — before ending up in the energy business, weather-stripping and plugging leaks in crummy suburban homes. I despised the routine of repetitive labor, chafed at long hours, realized there were limitations in my hands-on craftsmanship. My roommate at the time, training for secondary Earth Science, invited me a few weekends up to his family's cabin on Madeleine Island, surrounded by serene and limitless Lake Superior. With enough beer and sunshine, we beached three compelling reasons to be a teacher: *June, July,* and *August.*

My decision generated uncertainty. Even if I were able to overcome fears of speaking in public — and it became easier when my role was leader — would I be an *effective* teacher? Would I *enjoy* youngsters? Did I have the *raw ability?* Could I handle *every* detail and responsibility? Could I adjust to the *unyielding schedule?* In short, could I successfully return to a place I left in boredom and frustration only 10 years earlier? I felt befuddled by questions — probably similar to Peter, my former student. (And Mike, Amy, Kori and Jill, former students, now teachers or potential teachers all.) But I must insist that my decision wasn't based on knowing the right answer to any of them. I decided more on the basis of the process I would experience — a fact that my father, in all his intimate detachment, might particularly appreciate. The best way to deal with frightful monsters is to turn a light on, look them eye-to-eye. Pushing myself to lead groups would provide the kind of challenge I needed to become a fuller human being — even if it scared the shit out of me.

* * *

September, 1987, I was a student teacher sitting in the back of Mr. Dick's class for a month, barely saying a word, watching them plow through *Our Town,* do vocabulary, get started on Homer's *Odyssey.* Mr. Dick, a humanities instructor of long standing, could dominate class through sheer personality — reading a Burns poem in Scottish brogue, whining his voice like a child, sharing a derisive letter to be mailed to *60 Minutes*. An accomplished scholar with a barrel chest and lurking bravado, he was an unmovable force, 25 years of teaching and only occasional bouts of eating students alive. His files were thickened with worksheets, reading guides, true/false quizzes, unit reviews, multiple choice tests. Before they could graduate, every junior would have to run the gauntlet of Mr. Dick's literary steeplechase. "What did Odysseus' men slaughter contrary to wishes of the gods on the Island of the Sun?" "What witch turned his men to swine on their 4th adventure?" "Which weapons did they use to dispatch the suitors plaguing Ithaca?" Folder after folder, Chapter 1 to the end. The unfortunate double-entendre of his name was an open joke amongst students (duh?!), and with his serious glasses, thin hair and biting tongue, he was far more feared than loved.

As a graduate student at St. Thomas, student teaching for 10 consecutive weeks was my last hurdle before getting a license; it had landed me in Brooklyn Center, a tiny school district north of Minneapolis. Approximately 700 students spent 7th through 12th grade in the same, long-halled building, getting to know every jog and jut, hearing endless gossip, anticipating their long-awaited graduation. For my part, I was suffering from a tony background in the liberal arts. As an undergraduate at Carleton, I had devised a major in Comparative Literature studying the onset of Modernism in Western culture, reading novels in French, Spanish, English, a field which I realized only later attracts the most cerebral of academics.

This fascination of mine for getting a handle on issues of the modern world originated in 1977 in Vermont with Ms. Ayers, herself a superb teacher of high school humanities. She was an elderly woman whose face, in its simplicity, sadness and inscrutable down-turned lips, reminded me of a mime. I took her class entitled *Man and the 20th Century*. Her thesis started from the work of four giants — Einstein, Marx, Darwin and Freud — positing that a person's life had been made so unpredictable, so devoid of tradition, so fraught with absurdity and forces beyond control, that he (and I would imagine "she") had to scrape for meaning individually, without a social consensus, vulnerable to a withering disregard for human life. We read Kirkegaard, Kafka, Woolfe, Sartre, Camus, Joyce, Eliot and Pound. As she talked, she looked out the window, paused and seemed to measure some ultimate meaning, find the exact way of parsing it, as if small bits of wording tipped the balance between truth and mere apostasy. My academic skills blossomed beneath the rubric of examining such questions, discovering paths blazed by Western thought, knowing an authority out there cared what I believed and why.

I had the conviction as a student-teacher — however idealistic or uninformed — that learning and education were about this valorous search: to thrash through what life was for and what great — mostly white, European and male-writers had to say about it. (It was still the '70s!) That was the ultimate good of reading: it involved intense formulations, worthy debates, thought-out opinions. I believed the details of a story were secondary or tertiary to feelings, perspectives, themes. "Right" and "wrong," "true" or "false" were never part of my process of loving to read or think or write. I shook my head silently in the back as elegiac breakthroughs in *Our Town* got glossed over, students going through their meaning-starved days exactly as Thornton Wilder imagined: their voice screaming "Pathos!" throttled and reduced to its name, rank and serial number à la Mr. Dick.

On my first day, I introduced myself without much fanfare or elaboration. There was no particular panic, nor need for the restroom. I cleared the first hurdle. Now what? "I would like to start with a question which has intrigued me a long time. What is literature? I mean, that is what we are doing here in this class, reading literature, studying humanities, but what is it?" My voice was tenuous, but I exhibited energy and interest, my brows reaching upward like a suppliant. There were no audible groans, though a few heads fell into hands as they sideways eyed the clock, deliberating how much an hour a day for two months added up to. Mr. Dick fidgeted in the back, arms folded, seeming to say "Where are you going? What about getting back to *The Odyssey*? Chop-Chop!" Silence felt like a weight holding down my entire life, but not long. "It's like stuff that people write," Tom pitched in rather stiffly. A nice kid, friendly. One I had gotten to talk with. Not the stuff of Nobel Prizes, but a start.

"Just stuff?" I pressed.

"Literature is like feelings and thoughts of people written down." It was Tracy, in front, a cheerleader that fall. I didn't know enough to reward her small risk, perhaps risking so much myself, but I did pick it up and repeat it.

"Thoughts and feelings, written down. Okay. Mark?" Hands were popping up like idea kernels on a stove.

"It has to be famous people, like Shakespeare or *Hamlet*." I let that pass.

"I think it's just plays and poetry and novels that have been published." This was Julie, not terribly motivated but willing to chime in with the novelty of a discussion.

"So, why do we read them? I mean, there are a lot of things we could be doing with our time." "We don't" someone tossed, drawing snickers, but others paused, thought about it, debated. Later, I held up different sections of a newspaper, asking which ones constituted literature. There were news stories, a film review, an obituary page, an Ann Landers column, an editorial. They hemmed and hawed, argued some, found few clear answers but did, at least, engage. I wrote my best definition on the board: "Literature represents the written thoughts, feelings, values and/or perspective of a person from a given culture at a given time." My *litteratura* was nearly illegible, trailing off by five or six degrees, but to my surprise some students actually wrote this in their notebook: a hopeful sign. Mr. Dick looked on puzzled, scratching around his tightly buttoned collar, like — what was I doing to his ponies?

In truth, I was not entirely sure. In my teaching fantasy, I imagined leading a band of students down streets in Brooklyn Center — much as I had with Bookchin during the teacher's strike in high school — stopping traffic as huge banners demanding more and better literature pushed forward against tear gas and police lines. We would chant "Conrad! Conrad! Conrad!" outside an office-building until a beleaguered administrator showed up to answer. We would throw out the old guard and throw open the new, usher in the possibility that learning was fun, profound and changed lives.

Back in reality, I couldn't deliver much in the way of oratory or insight; or even well-structured activities. I remember that I wore a greasy pair of black slacks used for bussing tables in Vermont, tired sneakers and a paisley shirt that needed ironing. I was one year into training for a profession I hadn't given much thought to — especially in terms of pedagogy or wardrobe. There wasn't much I could offer. But I did communicate some improvisational notion that Humanities would be different now, more about discussion and producing ideas. And students — bless their hearts — came willingly along, as much because they felt liberated from a teacher with all the right answers as intrigued by a young man who had none.

* * *

April, 2000. I walk like a veteran teacher under graying hair, an odd comfort amidst teeming crowds of teenagers. In the lounge before school

I fill up a water bottle. It's a ritual, but also a necessity. Teachers are supposed to consume more than the recommended two quarts daily, but imagine how this complicates the smooth management of 5 different classes: basic bodily processes — going to the john, grabbing a bite, stepping out for air — necessarily have to wait, sometimes for hours. I wonder how many working professionals would put up with these limitations for the sake of a rugged crop of "Generation X-Y-Z." I stride purposefully out and make toward the office, wearing my teacher's shroud of invisibility through the kids. Americans hail the efficiency of business, how markets enforce a kind of discipline, but let's face it: most white-collar days allow much greater flexibility — a multitude of breaks, personal calls, e-mail, and lunches dressed as tax breaks which are a stretch-limo service compared to the 25 minute rickshaw-line of public school.

Naturally, there are exceptions. I hail Mr. Donne, the old dog sniffing around a coterie of associates just inside the office finishing up a round of stories, repeating the old saw: "Those who can, do; those who can't, teach." They all send up a roar. Not my favorite refrain. With teachers up and down my family tree, it cuts a little close to the trunk. I nod my head in the form of "Good Morning" but am unwilling to waste much time on small talk. It feels curious to me, though, because lately I have to admit I am more aware of how little technical expertise or marketable professional skills I actually possess.

I walk to my room secretly wondering what else I would do to make a living. I could retool if I had to: go back to school, maybe jump directly to technical writing, corporate training, or screening airport luggage. But as it is, I feel strained to my limit by old plumbing or completing income tax forms. The feeling that I don't have distinct abilities or in-depth knowledge makes me suppose I don't possess valuable skills. Not just in construction or engineering or hands-on healing, but with common, desirable things — making snappy computer presentations, creating tax shelters, appreciating the complexity of classical music. It may seem odd but old feelings of insecurity and incompetence still visit. Maybe the saw is true: teachers can't really "do" any one thing particularly well.

I wonder though now, if that isn't what allows teachers to be so effective. Like many professions, teachers are asked to execute a particular function within a larger operation — instructing biology, for example. The best will do that while all the time not "locking themselves in" in terms of their field or judgment about kids. Teachers are asked to facilitate a wide spectrum of personalities, topics and skill levels, instructing biological concepts as much and math abilities, effective English as much as helpful research techniques. They must do this for the college bound as well as those just learning English. A sensibility for gauging where students are at in relation to the material, and also to broader concerns, is what makes for an educator instead of just skating by as a mere instructor. Being a generalist is what allows for success across a broad spectrum of students and issues. I think of my strait-laced student Peter being able to reel in a rough-house like his buddy John — doing the work of managing personalities. Or his interest in knowing a little bit about everything back home, traffic to weather to sports, and how that helps to ground him and relate with others.

A good teacher's strength is more process than product; more about interest in learning and making it happen than clinging to the authority of knowledge. Even in a very tangible field like biology, the best teaching does not consist chiefly of imparting particular or specific truths as much as assisting at the birth of curiosity and interest in the minds of others — more mid-wife than god. It requires connectedness, a full sensibility for intangibles, the kind of equanimity which might be lacking in a highly directed or decisive individual: one who feels bored, frustrated or diminished waiting for less developed students to make a breakthrough. This openness to process means that small details and observations flow in from seemingly irrelevant sources only to be applied later as the perfect patch-work in reaching out to a kid or driving home a point.

Most important, a good teacher is never disappointed at starting over or re-teaching because beginning again is foundational to education. It's how we do our work: one little piece balanced on top of the other — an impossible stacking-dishware trick — hoping it holds together. If they fall down, we start over. Teachers start over anyway: every year, every trimester, every class period, always cheerful (hopefully) and with the same goal in mind. In so doing, we allow a larger reality to settle in around the room: Truth happens. All the time. Every instant. The job of teaching is about opening yourself to that remarkable perspective, not retreating behind a known body of facts.

* * *

That Mr. Donne in the office is much different than me: a handy guy, competent in numerous ways; he could even install a new bathroom if he had to. Near retirement after 30-some years, he knew down to an exact number the days and class periods left. He even worked up a separate career tending bar at night. Truly affable, with thick features and warm smile, eyebrows pushing the center of his forehead, he could carry a conversation himself. You wanted to trust him. Custodians, administrators, lunch-ladies, and a lot of students did, though he definitely preferred adults. He began teaching in the late '60s and loved telling jokes, the dirtier and racier the better.

Invariably, after the bell rang, you found him languidly stirring coffee in the lounge or chatting up staff in the office; his classes wouldn't start for 10 or 15 minutes yet. In the years since smoking was eliminated, he would go out driving in his car and come back with a mint in. Students did little or no work in class, the vast majority receiving an "A" for not saying much about it. They wrote occasional papers, gave short presentations quickly evaluated, slugged their way through multiple-choice exams which Donne carefully went over the day before. He was unable or unwilling, at this point, to do much real instruction. Learning, ideas, inspiration, that was up to students. He was a "practical English teacher" and instructed how to fill out job applications or write resumes. He used to brag in the lounge how if the school district initiated action against him that very day, with all the due process and union procedures, unless he committed a felony on school grounds, it would take five years to be removed. He laughed and laughed, only two years from full retirement.

The most intriguing thing is that Mr. Donne had more student-teachers work under him than anyone. Apparently his expertise was in high demand. He had a good relationship with a local Christian college, most years working with two new teachers, one in fall, one in spring. This meant that Mr. Donne did even less during those trimesters — spending hours reading in the lounge or making calls from the English office. Of course, he did put some time in, assuring, reassuring his charges that everything about class was completely normal and to be expected. "I think you're doing just fine. Right on schedule, really." Meetings with the overtaxed college professor came off without a hitch. He faithfully took each student-teacher's photo, adding them to a little poster in our office, everyone of them holding a book artificially at a desk in the library.

Of the many troubling issues in public education, selectively thinning out dead wood — or even just ineffective staff — is not among the most hotly debated. Nor is how we go about teacher recruitment and training. There are academic articles, proposals, even fads, but in truth, the "standards" movement, investments in technology, a fight over vouchers and ongoing budget dilemmas have sucked the air out of education discussions. Occasionally, you read how, because of a wave of retirements, America will need 1 million new teachers by the year 2012. "Why thin the herd?" is one sentiment. Retaining any kind of experienced staff is a positive during rapidly changing times. Ditto with teacher training programs. Education colleges gladly accept most every student who comes their way. It's not like getting into med school or a law program; even veterinarians have a far tougher course to negotiate than instructors of that more advanced mammal.

No doubt a number of teachers, like Mr. Donne, exhibit symptoms of burnout, but here is my question: How does a person in any field maintain a creative outlook and passion, day after similar day, year after repetitive year? Certainly, there are countless working Americans in the same boat, but the devastating point is this: Given their line of work, their personal motivation and effectiveness is not that important to us. (Even George W. Bush, in discussing his dubious National Guard service, was able to hold off critics by claiming gamely: "I put my time in.") In other words, in what other profession does your effectiveness, or just your matter-of-fact non-chalance, impact so many that it becomes a regular issue for editorialists and politicians seeking higher office? We must realize that the constant carping and hand-wringing over teachers and public education under-scores emphatically how crucial this job is — how desperate we really are to find more and better. Yet, it is much more disturbing and depressing that none of this has resulted in significant changes in how education happens, how teachers are recruited or compensated, how the vast majority of schools are structured.

Educational research, along with something I intuitively trust more — my own anecdotal observations — suggest only one in 10 experienced educators continue to blossom in later years, becoming truly masterful, capable of inspiring students as well as training novices. Two such teachers, one in art, one in health education, retired the year after Mr. Donne. Each was a prime example of having changed lives, putting their will to the service of others, fashioning themselves into giants in their field. They were wonderful characters, wise, wry, friendly with kids. They also each mentored teaching candidates who taught and got hired in our district. This is the way education is supposed to work and occasion-ally does.

During Donne's last year, I visited with a parent whose son had moved from my class as a junior where he earned average grades in Mr. Donne's class as a senior. She believed this was the best thing that ever happened to him. In my class, he struggled with the complexity of issues and didn't demonstrate interest or skill in writing or thinking. Now as a senior, everything had changed. Relaxed, he felt confident about himself and his abilities, held down an outside job, made good grades and most importantly, was set to graduate on time. His relationship with the jovial, unprepossessing English teacher was working magic. Where I had failed by asking too much, he found a comfortable niche where he was doing just fine as he was.

We need to ask fundamental questions here: How many students want a rigorous program and academic challenge? How many would be excited to fool with really profound questions in high school? How many would prefer just to waltz through with a credible record but no real affinity or passion for learning? Get to a junior college and from there look for a surer, safer career harbor? There aren't easy answers, and invariably, if you fix on the paradoxes of education instead of relationships, they will take you around and around while the needs of students stand still. It's not ideal but in the process of working a career, any given teacher might blossom into an abundant canopy inspiring crowds or wither into a spindly cactus without so much as a useful shadow. The same is true of students. I've seen both. It is hard to say how it's going to go in advance, and even harder to determine who cares enough about it to maneuver the process more one way than the other.

There was another teacher in the same field and age-group as Mr. Donne that I watched over years, Mrs. Wright. She was short, with a pre-World War II type body, old-fashioned hair, thick glasses and taught in many different buildings. (Like abusive priests, there are ways to fob teachers off on other schools.) She did not have a commanding presence with her sparse, crackling voice; her methods were antiquated (she gave regular spelling tests) and her classes were frequently out of control, a grab-bag of comments, groans, laughter. Looking out behind glasses with steady brown eyes was a person who watched, cared and listened as if these were her own. She moved slowly, shared salty opinions, went about business without taking herself too seriously, and that was just fine with students. No deadlines. Again, like Mr. Donne, not much of an academic workout. She was treated by colleagues as somewhat of an embarrassment: the crazy basement aunt that no one wants to have for supper.

During winter one year, I noticed that there would be three girls sitting on the floor outside Mrs. Wright's room. They had books with them, novels, but they mostly talked leisurely, copied work or doodled.

I asked them once why they were always in the hall during class. "Oh, it's too noisy in there for us to concentrate. She just gives us time to get our work done." There was a circus-y kind of din leaking steadily from behind the door. Hmm. I understood. My classes felt noisy at times too. Not my place.

Interestingly, when she and Mr. Donne retired recently, I noticed how many students were truly touched by their relationship with each teacher. Tears, hugs and heartfelt cards filled their last week in the building. After 30 some years, a time span that witnessed America's transition from industry to information, Mrs. Wright's and Mr. Donne's ships had come in. They were not paragons of instructional excellence. Over three decades, there were definite things that changed in education, and neither had absorbed or applied any of it. But there were also things which stayed the same: students need a person who accepts them, gives them a place to be themselves. Process, not product. Both of them had found a way to make theirs work, however unevenly, even if they didn't always have to themselves.

* * *

Observing what goes on in school, listening to what parents and students say, has taught me that in the very complex process between human beings we call education, it is subjective and risky to judge a teacher's effectiveness, pedagogy or philosophy. Obviously, we want teachers to be better than average; but also, they can do worse than the ancient saying "Above all, do no harm." I am afraid we are embarking today on an educational experiment — standardized and uniform testing — that has potential for great harm, especially in the hands of inexperienced teachers. I am wary of critics who have the right answers, distrust dogmatic reformers promising to wring greater "efficiency" from schools as if they were factories. (Rod Paige, Secretary of Education under George W. Bush recently made just such a comparison, writing glowingly in a letter to *The New Yorker* on the genius of Henry Ford's assembly line concept.)

My hands have been full — literally tied — with responsibilities in my room, and while I would like to believe I dealt effectively with most students, there were some that I just did not reach. Some moments I am totally elated by this work, at others completely deflated. At times I am clear on my mission and how to get there, at others, I feel fogged in. This is how I gauge it when I say that teaching is an entirely "human" profession — that it is the process which must govern. From the very first person in the door to the last out at night, education conforms to needs and realities of actual people, not demands put on it by political or bureaucratic establishments several steps removed.

It would be wrong-headed to believe only some teachers know what they are doing and never falter, while others are clever imposters robbing children of an education, feeding at the public trough. The truth, if anyone ever finds it, is more elusive and short-lived. Educators worth even a half-handful of salt face a certain simple reality, the same one Peter and I asked ourselves undertaking such a challenging experience: "Can I really do this, day in and day out?" There is no good way to fake it or cheat. Teachers want to have a positive and meaningful impact and they give it a good shot, at least for awhile. No one considers what happens years down the line when sensitivity and inventiveness start to wane; no one knows where the process will lead.

Certainly, salary is a major issue for attracting young teachers and mid-career professionals seeking change. Standard thinking holds that greater pay attracts greater quality. But the bare truth is, no one can inspire a person to be a teacher like another teacher. Not money, not June-July-August, not little children with lost expressions on their face. Like a kind of religion, you have to feel it before you can believe it. A Socrates leads to Plato leads to Aristotle, and so on. Still more troubling, almost nothing can ensure that a person today will stay in education for 20 or 30 years like the Mr. Donne's or Ms. Wright's, not even an inspiring first teacher like Socrates. We are slipping toward "mediocrity," as the 1983 report, *A Nation at Risk* posited, but for reasons other than listed then. Not just by virtue of losing good (and average) people to retirement, or because of wasted time and resources on standardized testing, or even in the under-enticement of qualified candidates, but because the ethos of a single lifetime career has been supplanted by frequent shifting in and out of occupations. As we lose that critical mass of inspiring veteran teachers, cross over the tipping point of instructional excellence, the result means fewer and fewer good students ever think about becoming teachers in the first place.

And for once, I do have an answer. Believe it or not, after everything I said about process, I honestly believe it is the *one right answer*. Here is what should be done about public education in America: We should replace teacher unions with subject-specific teacher firms which operate in similar fashion to law firms, handling one subject in a school's educational program. The school board would grant teaching contracts with individual firms to provide their district services in "science" say, or "math," or "English." These firms would be responsible for training members, advancing senior staff to positions of authority and merit, assessing quality, keeping abreast of developments. In short, teachers would acquire responsibility for maintaining membership, excellence and compensation in their respective firms. School administrators would get out of the business of monitoring teachers and evaluating them, which most are not very good at, and get back to dealing with infractions, public relations, the physical plant and budgeting.

The free market enters in the form of teaching firms competing for district contracts which might come up every two, three or four years. Good firms would command good contracts and at times have to hire and train more teachers. School districts would be able to make changes in emphasis, from a back-to-basics type firm to one that stresses cooperative learning or student-driven projects. The kinds and quality of firms would likely multiply rapidly, providing parents with real choice and options in regard to their district's educational strategy, albeit mediated by school board decision. For once, we might actually ask kids what they want and prefer or whether a group of teachers should be retained. Instead of one-size-fits all, school programming would become adaptable, innovative, diverse, much like the rest of American culture. We would inject vitality into the search for effective strategies and curriculum. As important, within teaching firms you have a natural system of senior mentors and junior partners: people on the way out who can consolidate a lifetime of skills into mentoring; people on the way up who want to learn more and see opportunities to make a career of it.

A straight-forward, radical, yet practical program that would eliminate much of the tension between teachers and administrators. A sure-fire system for rewarding good educators, weeding out bad and continuously attracting new candidates. Teachers would have extra incentive to serve and impress management with their professionalism. There is no doubt in my mind this would work. But, of course, it is unlikely to ever happen. As with so many great ideas in education, an idea is not enough. You see, for all their reliance on standardized tests with single, correct answers, the education establishment does not actually live in a world where a right answer makes any difference. The system is mired in process, too: collective bargaining, politics, interfacing with local, state and federal agencies and, of course, convincing the taxpaying public that this whole system actually works. They make kids do it but cannot hold themselves accountable *to finally get education right.*

If I haven't already, I need to make something clear: school districts and unions, this great two-headed monster engorging itself around the task of teaching kids, are not capable of reforming themselves, just as politicians are incapable of sincerely restructuring or devolving power. There is too much money sloshing through holds and galleys of this mammoth vessel, ensuring that it is in too many people's interest to allow the system to just float along, leaking as it goes, expensive bilge pumps running full-time below deck. For every instructor who has lost her passion and purpose for teaching, there are at least as many who have found secure employment somewhere in the education establishment. Sadly, major reform will not happen while these two bureaucracies are piloting the ship. It is clear from their concerns and actions that children are not their top priority.

Our educational system demands right answers and accountability to satisfy *their own fear* of the future, not to enhance young people's efficacy. It is much more about *their world* than kids. Our children are the brave ones: willing to start out a career and raise a family, head down to the university and take up a major, sit through an English class to clear the path to college. We are the weaklings, the adults in charge: absorbed with work, constantly preoccupied, fearing the worst about our children's future and through wrong-headed obsessions, making sure we get it. And then we justify this by spending huge sums of money to administer tests which prove scientifically that, in fact, our children's education, *which we are responsible for*, is "measurably" bad.

* * *

Amazingly, none of this has a very profound effect, as far as I know, on preventing people from going into teaching. (The real kettle of fish, like I say, is how long teachers stay: half are gone in just five years!) Teachers are like the Hydra in Greek mythology; cut off one head, 10 more spring up to replace it. There is that steady turn out every fall, enough bodies, licensed or not, good, bad or dispirited, to get the job done. It is a "job," after all, though virtually every teacher hopes they are the exact person who, despite all obstacles, finds a way to make an important difference in a kid's life. Most of them became teachers to answer a calling in their heart: an ideal, often stretching back nostalgically to instructors of their youth. Unfortunately, too many experience a let-down once they get there, realizing that administrative burdens, classroom management and overall demands for energy more than trump their feeling of connection with kids.

Teachers are asked, as Parker Palmer has noted, to "stand where the personal and the public meet," to use their personal experience and integrity as a tool for drawing in any and all of the public's children. What we need to realize is that it is an *internal striving* to succeed that is the enduring mark of a great teacher; their drive emanates from an *internal focus* and thus is not something the educational system can easily reproduce or even knows how to support. A good teacher is made not by the system, but through an almost conspiratorial confluence of personal factors, familial and experiential, accidental, trivial and profound. And in fact, today, as the delicate public-personal balance shifts, requiring more public liability — burdensome testing, increased class sizes, greater needs among students — and less personal fulfillment, even good teachers are leaving in droves. Many go in with an open heart only to desert when they realize what the public asks them to do with it.

Like any profession, though, if it is yours to do, it will find a way to feed you. Working to transform the lives of children can be enormously rewarding. It has been for me. But seeing education in those terms presupposes that you yourself recognize the value of transformation, perhaps even, that you yourself have been transformed. That is my own bias, having been given up for dead as a public speaker. My "recovery" from failing at speaking has kept me sensitive and focused on the core challenge of education: the need to grow personally as a human being. This is the true mission of learning and being alive. I feel its power daily. And yet, sadly, in the vast majority of classrooms we are sentencing young students to endless drills and repetition, not helping them with important personal challenges or putting these into a context which makes them meaningful. In seeing young people merely as unknowing and in need of programmatic education, we diminish responsibility for their own learning and wanting to improve their own lives.

Maybe teachers want to teach not because they "can't do" but because they "can see" the value in helping others get beyond ignorance or unskillfulness to a better place, as if their own journey has been centered all along on overcoming a particular set of deficiencies. I believed that myself when I had just the puniest ability to bring light into a room: convincing myself it was a worthwhile pursuit as long as I could help *one* person, change *one* life other than my own. I created each lesson, conducted every class, graded each paper by sinking my best self into it, almost all of this on instinct: learning tricks, sharpening focus, finding ways to gain entry into students' kitchens where I could rattle pots and pans as easily as settle them to a cup of tea. Teaching became a way of making myself useful, ensuring that daily work added up to something commensurate with my love and understanding of the world. I never figured on getting this far or going this deep. And I can't reach into my memory for a particular incident, a funny class or an unusual kid without another dozen coming out and falling in my lap where I have no idea what to make of them. Happily, any time a scrap of feedback or evidence of success came my way, I opened a file drawer and threw it in a folder. I have since bound these notes and photos and cards into a kind of scrapbook to remind myself that, in fact, I did achieve my goal. And then some.

Most educators don't appear phased by tides and cycles in teaching, returning every fall with more in their briefcase, beginning anew, taking another shot. They pack the past skillfully away. There is no way of knowing where teaching will lead, and it feels intimidating not knowing. It has for me. Years later, I can say that it turned out well, that eventually I did get it right; but even when I didn't — not to worry — students moved ahead anyway as we all do, pushing forward to meet life's demands. Our children are smart enough, as we were, to know what to take, what to leave at school; their natural instincts and passions roll on despite our best efforts to stifle them.

I've come to appreciate something crucial about teaching and the impetus for learning: it's better to concentrate on and value the process. If for no other reason than to acknowledge that the product, like ourselves, will never be entirely finished.

Part II:
Teacher in Residence

aissatou angel

Over years, I built a routine; really, several routines within a large wheel of routine. There was the daily one: waking, getting to school, preparing, teaching, having lunch, finishing up, heading home to nap, work out, make dinner. But there was also a weekly one, Monday to Friday, which, because of dwindling energy reserves and students' cresting exuberance, I worked as its own mini-unit — building to an activity Friday which required maximum involvement by students, minimum output from myself. In addition, there were lengthy seasonal routines, each linked to a familiar pattern — the long, sensual send-up of autumn (going back to school), a staunch obliteration of Minnesota's landscape in winter (Christmas vacation), the sudden opening of new ground in March (spring break) and the verdant overgrowth of June (end of school) which students prize as epic and unlimited. In between large and small cycles, there were others tied to professional tasks: the routine of novels, of units, of marking periods, of ending and starting classes, and over years, of seeing students come in one end, go out the other.

The existence of so many routines is what lures educators and students into a kind of dull uniformity. The sameness of it erodes any sense of unique experience, overmasters the spontaneity of "here and now," the backbone of creativity. Our economy is geared to routine, to production schedules and efficiency, to each of us showing up at a fixed time because the whole world — or at least our paycheck — depends on it. And of course, routine is exactly what the public demands of school, so adults can leave mornings, come home from work, pick up their kid after practice and experience so little departure from normalcy that they have no need to discuss — *what happened? what's new? what did you learn?* — but simply flow into separate channels at home.

I have always hated routine. Being a student most often felt dreadful, boring, without the least stimulation. As a senior in Vermont, I wrote a lengthy expose for the local alternative paper, *The Vanguard Press*, decrying the blandness of high school, which read, in part:

> The daily routine, established in September and not completed until mid-June, repeats itself over and over, like a tireless merry-go-round spinning endlessly, carrying teachers and students in circles: the same class, at

the same time, in the same room, with the same teacher and the same kids, every day of the week of every month.

A big apprehension about becoming a teacher was whether I could withstand the pressure of being chained to a daily schedule like I remembered from high school.

My early years teaching went fine, fears receded and I settled in, though I did alter one aspect of my routine: arriving earlier to school every morning. No more mad dashes from the parking lot or frenzied negotiation of crowded halls prior to the bell. I had a solid hour, sometimes more, to sit at my desk, dither through details, handle crises and polish off preparations. I got tons more done in the morning hush than the chaotic free-for-all which followed. And I was not alone: other teachers, wise ones, were already in the building. It seems there is always a handful who wake before alarms go off — avoiding one bell — their energy pointing to getting in early as just the right push toward a great day.

* * *

I first met Aissatou (ice-a-too) on one of those early mornings at school. She was walking awkwardly with help from a pair of metal hand crutches, looking raw and scared, her American mom making sure she visited every classroom on her schedule. Aissatou was from West Africa, had only just arrived, just barely, from the dilapidated village of her homeland, where she left her mom and dad and siblings. She had pictures and showed me them, introduced in slow, monotone English. I jumped to French at one point and her face brightened, words flowed easier, her mom seeming confident about prospects of her new daughter finding a home here.

Aissatou was born with club feet, walking only with the greatest difficulty. Her American parents belonged to a church and did relief work. They would regularly take on cases, bring children to the States, get them treatment, perhaps see them into college. It wasn't government; I don't think it was even about religion; for them, it was helping people with no means, one at a time — a concept I appreciated. And here she was, fresh from Africa, 16 years old, thin as a rail, with dark braided hair and deep brown eyes more open to the world than ever. She would be in my sophomore American literature class, for two periods every other week. She promised to do her best and learn English.

81

That first meeting made no large impression. I can't say I went out of my way in early weeks to make Aissatou feel well-adjusted or at home. I smiled a lot, dropped French on her, ascertained that she was getting to class on time with her unusual gimp-legged gait. The fact is that the first weeks are a blur of faces and fast bells, new and old students mixed, kids switching in or out, some that never show up. I have to meter out finite energy where instinct tells me it's needed. Aissatou never made the radar screen; a good sign.

As fall wore on, the routine of being back at school held sway, and so did Aissatiou's presence. Her English improved. Though still heavily accented, I noticed how she was able to laugh more, took notes, visited regularly with group mates. She also turned in assignments, and they tended to be well thought out, though printed in an idiosyncratic *internationale* script. I scored her well but detected the hand of her American mother in this, especially after an administrator showed up one day with an unsolicited e-mail:

> I'm really impressed with the curriculum and assign-ments in Aissatou's English/Social Studies Class. It was really worth reorganizing her schedule so that she could have this class. The types of assignments are designed to stimulate critical thinking and clear verbal expression and will be very helpful for her educational and personal development. And my brief interactions with Mr. Henry and Mr. Hunt have shown genuine warmth and interest in Aissatou and her education.

It felt odd to be garnering praise from a parent so quickly and unex-pectedly; even odder to realize we were being monitored. (Though there were mistakes: she got my name right but not my partner — Lund, not Hunt — a fact worth laughing about even today.)

Sophomores are required to give frequent presentations, and I knew that for Aissatou this represented an important challenge. Still, I could not have imagined that during her second speech, she would suddenly seize-up and lower her head to the lectern when she lost her way. I was momen-tarily without words myself, waiting, waiting, waiting at my desk, but eventually ventured encouragement, asked if she wanted to start over, and, upon seeing no movement or signs of life, went over the day's details and dismissed class to the library. It went beyond five minutes, well past her time limit, and she remained firmly pressed to the lectern. *What an odd thing*, I thought: frozen as if in a trance. I left a small group of young women in the room and accompanied class to the library, where, after another 10 minutes, they showed up with Aissatou and no particular trauma to report. I have no idea what exorcism they performed; nor did I show much concern or speak to her about it — pretending it happens all the time. Though I did call her mom to compare notes, and ask her to be furtive, downplay any significance Aissatou might assign to the glitch.

Later that week, Aissatou tried again and did just fine, her slow monotone stepping through English in the measured way she had practiced at home. There was no getting lost or floundering. The class cheered roundly and I never saw another hint of trouble. Over months she showed up at times in my room, before school or after, asking questions about class work or more often, just chatting about school or home or life in America. Her way of talking seemed so formal, so dignified, as if petitioning a local chief on behalf of her village: "Mr. Henry, do you know that I have fallen behind in Math?" I always just smiled and listened.

Aissatou landed in a wheelchair later that year: the first of two operations on her feet. And she also reenlisted in our team-taught program as a junior with many of the same students. She spent most of that year rolling to class in a motorized chair (she had the second operation), took the elevator up and down, her delicate pink backpack over the seat like a style statement on disability. The experience was marvelous, for her, for me, for all of us. She added to our discussions of Africa, kept up with our down-to-earth sense of humor, impressed with her desire to learn. It was great having her in class, but in truth, she was only one member of an otherwise excellent set — gregarious girls and charming young men — most helpful, eager, on their way up, a wonderful bunch to be a part of. Our approach to instruction built up over years, cooperative, engaging, personal, was working well. And a crippled young lady from the dirt-tracks of Africa was proving a good fit with the mainstream of an American high school.

That spring, I sat in my back yard at a picnic table reading through portfolios. End of year grading and a final summative letter to students: another routine. We had traveled far and wide, confronted Africa, hung with Buddhism, Daoism and Confucianism, walked the Western path all the way to the Americas. Time to say goodbye after two good years. Usually I plowed through portfolios without much self-awareness, giving credit here, extra points there. I simply confirm the overall worthiness of their efforts. These are their ideas after all, a record of their encounters with the profound and profane and everything in between; as long as they write and engage I'm pleased. But somehow I lost my disinterest at a certain point, lifted eyes from the page and marveled how these kids had grown. They weren't *my kids* in any sense; but then they were a lot more than mere students. Tears welled up like they had my last year at De La Salle; I was reading Aissatou's portfolio. Looking at how much she produced, the richness she found in discussing concepts or laying opinions to rest, I felt it tangibly, undeniably. The chicken scratch of a fledgling learner of English had blossomed into something strong, determined, beautiful, and I had been there to watch. As much as I was a part of her experience coming to America, she had grown to be a touching part of mine. And now an even larger cycle came into view, one just rounding the final turn after decades in the making: I could see the contours of my own emergence from a green, undisciplined student to a trusted mentor for young people. It was like I had been in training my whole life and only just then realized what it was for.

September of senior year Aissatou danced into my room without a chair or crutches or noticeable sign of impairment. "Lady Ice," I crooned with after-school friskiness. "Mr. Henry, look! I'm walking now. You know, I think I will go to the dance on Friday." She seemed so happy. I smiled, gave her a hug. Things were fine. Over the summer, she had returned to her family, visited old haunts, seemed more determined than ever to make medical school and return home as a pediatrician. Yes, I confirmed, how worthy. I looked forward to helping with college applications.

It wasn't about me, but around this time I grasped that working with kids meant finding a role to play, being a sturdy bridge, possibly a springboard, for their next thing. And that's what this work was — the classes, discussions, informal give-and-take, cluing in parents, important ideas, journals, recommendations, awards — the whole circus. It was all about them; nothing about me. Despite the vibrancy of my own young adventures, I determined to keep well-hid my life of training which fit the job I had to do. My life didn't matter. What did, was taking kids — as many as you can handle — and propelling them forward, challenging them, encouraging, praising, suggesting places to go. And not giving up — not on any, not ever — not unless you're willing to give up on creativity, regeneration, redemption. It is a supreme admission of failure to turn your back on someone so young, a failure which says more about you than the youngster. Even if you catch them stealing, lying, cheating or being unusually different, there is always another opportunity to be better, to do better, to come back to the center under new circumstances. At its core, that is what learning is really about: growing into something new, becoming someone better.

In its trying, overburdened way, being a teacher does add up, becomes greater than its sum of many parts. Unfortunately, that was only apparent to me after years in the trade. For a long time, I perceived only dimly that making a small difference to a kid on a daily basis was anything but routine.

a dozen things about teaching for five minutes

I f you've been with me up to here, this is where you will be tested, literally. The reality is, as much as we all care about children's education and future, when it comes to a close examination of school, like physically going there, almost no one does it. After 15 years in private and public schools, I can literally count on two hands the number of times an outside visitor, parent or not, came to observe class or just showed up. And I am someone who welcomes a visit any time and rarely, if ever, close my door on America's hallway.

In fact, a few years ago, Elvis stopped in — 6th period, African American Literature. I racked my brain trying to fit him in the discussion. He did dominate the airwaves at a crucial time, siphoning business from the gathering stars of Motown, though nothing like the Beatles. But then, the Beatles have never stopped by, not even at Halloween or Mardi Gras. I turned and there he was, leaning against the door jam, arms crossed like he has been doing this a long time. It was Las Vegas Elvis: white pants, ruffled shirt, black leather boots, side burns, overdone hair — everything but dark glasses. He looked a little short but we definitely got the idea.

"You don't even know me, do you Henry?" Elvis smiled, eyes beaming. I paused. There was something about him. I said he looked familiar which of course was no help: he looked familiar to everyone. "Gary Schultz, remember? Homeroom. We used to go at it. I was a pain-in-the-ass." He slowed down, gave extra purchase to "Pain-in-the-ass" so kids got the full flavor. I was goddamed if that wasn't exactly right. Little Garry Schultz. A manic kid. Up and down, ears like a donkey, got into fights, skipped class, hated school, just wanted out. Never did graduate. Now look at him. I couldn't call this success exactly, but he did real well singing "Love Me Tender," sweeping in front of girls, arms out. He never even took choir as far as I knew.

He told his story: how he kicked around California, got snared by drugs and alcohol, did rounds in underground fight clubs, whored and hustled, lost it all, then went into recovery. Always wanted to sing. Loved the hell out of Elvis. Now does competitions — 3rd place in Anoka. Women were all over him, but he's changed. Done with the haze of Graceland; brings a positive message now. He topped it with a two-minute punch and kick routine he trained himself with as a fighter — forcing breaths and snorts, executing several full splits, head-snaps at every turn and thrust, a lunatic on speed. *Remarkable,* I thought. We never got back on topic, a reason to keep your door closed, but it doesn't explain why, if someone as reclusive as Elvis makes it, the vast majority of parents, bureaucrats and politicians never do.

I want to take a tour, a short one, into high school. It will only last 5 minutes, but you'll learn enough about "the basics" to be well-informed the next time someone slick serenades you with an educational bill of goods.

* * *

It is 10:24 on a Wednesday morning, mid-September. I am outside my class in a moderate-sized suburb near Minneapolis. In theory, my task is to maintain control over the masses swinging by on the second floor: provide presence and a pair of eyes should anything go down. In reality, I am a poor excuse for a patrol, handing out smiles, hellos, head nods, more one of them than an authority figure like Mr. Baker down the hall, who at 57 is soldiering another day home. He's a competent lecturer in history and pretty much cares about each kid, but any departure from his routine of lectures, films, exams, and poster board projects is not in the cards. He sits kids at separate desks to inhibit conversation and interaction. There is way too much material he needs to cover to allow for discussion or debate. More than once he's told me that the key to getting cooperation in class is to never smile before Christmas; a rule he occasionally violates. One year on final-exam day in June (yes, the door was open), I spied a mirror taped to his blackboard. A sign read: "Person to see if you are unhappy about your grade." I guess you could say he's old school.

For better or worse, we work this wing as a kind of far-flung detachment: mall security without training, equipment or close back-up. (Personally, I am glad he used to coach wrestling and knows a few good holds.) These hallways are most congested immediately after the bell, troops heading out — lunch for some, others facing another hour of hard time before their reprieve from American education. The mixing of young bodies lends itself to both extreme connection and acute misunderstanding. Here is a first lesson: *the jam-packed mix of America's halls*, the jostling, hugs, holds, handshakes, shrieks and bedlam. This is a condensed image of America's new blend, the 21st century mix. The 90s brought nothing if not another wave of hopeful immigrants looking for a place amidst the crowd — white, black, Asian, Hispanic, wealthy, poor, and all manner of mixed race, mixed attitude, mixed up youngsters. Take it as you will — the gemstones, rough-cuts and karmic-ly challenged; this is the raw material teachers work with, what dirties our hands, tries our soul. What we live and die for.

In some ways, not a lot has changed since the Mr. Bakers of the world first cut their teeth on young students. Two muscle-bound boys are discussing football quarterbacks as they stroll toward Economics; a girl with streaked make-up shouts "Call me!" to her friend; a veteran couple embrace in front of the reality they will not see each other for almost an hour. Shabby, stained carpeting runs the length of the corridor. It has been replaced once, unlike the crummy acoustic tile ceilings and bland wall coatings that give the unmistakable feel of a public institution. This school was built with tax money to provide the basics, not with any intention of inspiring. It's here for the sober, unremarkable purpose of housing children while adults dress and prepare them for the world out there.

In other ways, of course, everything has changed. The clientele, which was exclusively white until 1980, is now composed of 45 percent students of color, mainly African-American and Asian. Non-English conversations are commonplace. Personal styles, ranging from tattoos and piercings to sweat pants and religious scarves, from muscle shirts and exposed drawers to dangling pagers and cell-phones, have exploded as much as America's ethnic diversity. Just the fact we are post-Colombine, post *Nation At Risk*, post-measurable standards, post-technological revolution (read: surveillance cameras at every turn), means the dreamy high school days of yore have been pushed aside to combat mediocrity, isolation, criminality and tragedy. This comes home, intense and personal, when you catch yourself considering what to do if gunfire erupts from down the hall. A tired hand rakes the back of your head, "First thing, go check with Baker."

The year before, I walked into a bathroom in January before lunch, finding a young man removing shoes, lifting his feet one-at-a-time into the sink where water was running. "Washing up, huh?" I moved in next to him. He seemed surprised but not embarrassed (teachers rarely use the student restroom). I figured he was just in gym class or maybe from a poor family. "Yes," he enjoined after a bit, "it is time to pray." The student, well-composed, appeared fastidious, though wearing a typical American jogging combo. It was Ramadan, and now it made sense: cleanse before retreating to sanctuary. Bring to Allah the gift of grace, which in this case, could be done just off the library. And it's not only Muslims need for prayer that defines a new reality. Christians meet before school to pray and sing, Ethiopians gather to talk politics after school, kids without moms or dads get free breakfast, the nurse strategizes about whom to notify in cases of abuse or pregnancy, the school cop now has a special "holding room." For me, high school was never like this.

I am about to start sophomore English — English 10. Same kids. Same time. Every day. (On second thought, my high school was exactly like this.) Nothing could seem less remarkable as students file in with all the joy and expectancy of prisoners headed to a rock pile: slumped shoulders, heads down — trudge, trudge, trudge. They have mastered what we teach. *Reality number two: So much life in the hallway, so little makes it through the door.* What are we doing to stifle, evade and ignore kids' natural inclination to enjoy, celebrate and engage with learning? I nod silently to a trio of passing seniors who smile acknowledgement of time together last year in World Literature. Lakeisha, a talkative young woman who loves and lives for debate; Mark, a quiet, respectful young man with a slight stutter interested in law enforcement; Amy, a not-so-bright but tall, slender student who, if it works out, will move to California to try modeling. They are within reach of their immediate objective: graduating from high school, which in this community is not unremarkable. Their friendly eyes mean enough to me about being someone they trust, especially because most students are blank, indifferent, looking down so eyes never meet. It lets me know they care, and more importantly, that they appreciate care to begin with.

I'm not completely sure how or when "basic" learning like this happens, but I do know — above everything else — it is crucially important that kids build this foundation: an ability to care about their world, their life, their education. If they care about what they are doing, who their friends are, what happens to them, they are more than half way to being successful. I know this is connected to developing relationships, not just with a teacher and the material, though both are critical, but also with other students. Parent involvement is vital to student learning because it speaks of a caring relationship at home. Thinking back over my own experience makes it plain: I started from scratch in high school, only engaging when I believed there was something worthwhile involved. As relationships mattered, so did what happened in class or after school at practice.

It's so simple. Education should not be the mystery it is. Successful learning comes down to a productive relationship, or multiple relationships, between human beings. It's not sexy or subject to reliable measurement or even easily replicated. A teacher attempts to transmit something important and meaningful, perhaps trivial or mundane, but it is only possible through mutual acceptance of relationship, a most basic umbrella, which begins with caring. It happens best when the basis of that relationship is what students call "respect," or educators refer to as "genuine concern," but which I would argue is based upon compassion. "Love" really, the ultimate frontier of caring. Only love allows a teacher to cut through all of the crap, administrative, societal, even interpersonal, and find a way to touch a student personally, intellectually, meaningfully. *That's lesson number three* in our visit. Put it down in capital letters and underline it in bold strokes. *Effective teaching is all about love and modeling real care.* Care for the world, care for your material, care for that one kid who is your personal pain-in-the-ass, like Gary Schultz.

Whatever measure the public takes for effectiveness, whether of test scores, drop-out rate, class size, or per-pupil expenditure, this essential fact of human transfer and relationship as the basis of education will not change, will never change, no matter how much variety in skin color increases, whether students' noses sport rings or fish-hooks, whether funding falls through the floor or goes through the roof. The real issue is always a relationship between teacher and student; and because one is adult, specially trained and solely responsible for the other's learning, the quality of that teacher. Educational studies confirm, time and again, the single greatest influence in a child's education is the quality of teacher in his or her classroom, and by extension, the quality of their relationship. Don't rush it, don't ignore it, don't underestimate it and don't forget it. In fact, just take some time to think back and remember your own part and place in it. *Noble Truth number four: education is about relationship and transfer, one human being to another, as slow or fast as needed.*

* * *

The bell rings and there is a final rush throught the door and buzzing around tables. Kids love to break down and overrun the logic of bells. Nicole snatches the bathroom pass and rushes out. Tom, a Vietnamese kid, stands chatting in front of Lori's table; she is mature with long hair and works as a cashier at the same grocery store. Anita, a cheerleader, analyzes picks for Homecoming and lobbies group mates as to who to vote for. Mark and Bobby muse together over the design of the Mack truck on Mark's English notebook which, after four weeks, has yet to suffer even a pencil scratch. Josh, tall, oddly dressed, with rough skin, is wedged between Ashley and Kori, who are trying to repress laughter. Other students pull out folders and books, some are noiselessly digesting the graded papers on their tables; Amy is one of these, a sweet but very quiet Korean girl, adopted. Her eyes move quickly from face to face, betraying what she feels inside. There are 30 students here, as is typical, all unique and original; an incalculable tangle of abilities, hopes, dreams, foibles, weaknesses and insecurities.

A big part of the task is to capture as many as you can, hold them in ransom for their best effort, make them believe it is all crucial, then set them free like Lakeisha, Mark and Amy to become their own butterflies. How this gets done is up to the teacher: his or her individual will, experience and character. What hangs on walls, how furniture is arranged, whether students interact, how they are addressed, what material is read, how often they write or do homework, and what form evaluations take. This is all at the discretion of the person in charge, which today, in this room, means me. For one hour, I represent the community's hopes and dreams for these children's educational experience; I wouldn't want it any other way.

I take my work seriously — or comically as needed — prepare my lessons well, but ironically, almost anything and everything we cover today will soon be forgotten and discarded for all time: Emerson, Whitman, Thoreau, Chief Joseph, Frederick Douglass, colonialism, transcendentalism, the Harlem Renaissance, and likely, any understanding of the main thrust in this class: exploring America's journey and complex character. Even by the relatively proximate time these green, undeveloped students are seniors, they will remember only enough to smile and nod like Lakeisha, Mark and Amy, content to have been challenged, to have grown.

And yet, in an odd way, I must proceed as if everything I do, from the way I call on them, to methods I use to deliver a lesson, to the meaning I pluck from our story, is absolutely essential. Not because any of it is in isolation, but because all of it is: from having a safe, productive place to be to having a defined role in a group; from having the opportunity to speak, listen and share to watching an adult interact with children; from seeing a person passionate about what they do to knowing someone at school really cares about them. I cannot explain it with greater precision, and I am never quite sure if it makes sense or is widely understood: everything done in class today evanesces, will eventually go lost or forgotten — if ever understood in the first place — and that doesn't make a shred of difference. What matters is the actual experience, the feelings, impressions and attitudes created within each student. For lack of a better expression and to echo a previous theme: it's not the material but the process that matters. At least, that's what every ounce of intuition, instinct and experience tells me.

I step to the podium for my first official act: taking attendance. This is not a great way to inaugurate a relationship, but for all practical purposes as a professional, is the only requirement I must complete. It is the one way I communicate on the class' progress to the administration and for which, short of some flagrant crime, I can be held to any account. Whomever I mark absent will need a satisfactory explanation as to why they were gone. If they can't produce one, they will be given an "unexcused" absence (as opposed to "excused"), which can be used to reduce their grade by a one third increment (e.g. A- to B+), and which, if they accumulate beyond three for the period, will (theoretically) result in them being dropped from class and potentially, if that happens in enough classes (over half), high school altogether. It is all theoretical because for every strict attendance policy there are loopholes, exceptions and gray areas, not to mention massive bureaucratic headaches down in the office where proper parental notification, due process and political cover occupies a devastating amount of highly paid professional time.

Children learn from everything we do, including the enforcement of this policy. They learn that it is arbitrary, unforgiving, relentless — kind of like most adults. They also learn that their parents, or any reasonable facsimile, can take care of these issues by calling or writing. (Their word is somehow worth more.) After awhile, it becomes an unfortunate truth that what we frequently measure with attendance is co-dependency within a family unit: the ability of a child to win parents over to manipulating the system. At any rate, even if the student is removed from class, suspended or ultimately expelled, the school district is still 100 per cent liable for providing that child's education at home or in another location. It will cost more to do it, and in the vast majority of cases, the results will be less effective.

Here is Introduction to *High School Reality Lesson number five: if you are one of those who supports "back to basics", let's-get-tough-with-kids, traditional education, or you have an administrator who does, you are well on your way to accomplishing something notable:* 1) while establishing deterrence for students who might miss class, you have communicated that learning is not about inspiration, but coercion; 2) you have alienated a majority of kids from the institution you hoped would transform them; 3) you have assured that marginal students will not succeed in large percentages; and; 4) you have sentenced your most at-risk kids to almost certain failure, isolation and expulsion. Tough lessons here for everyone. But you know what? That's acceptable, because this policy is not about students; *it is about adults, and what most suits them.* Call that *lesson number six.* Adults have an extreme need to know where kids are; that they are safe and not out torching garages or blunts or making babies, at least between the hours of 7:30 a.m. and 2:00 p.m. when people are paid with tax money to watch them.

The underlying rationale here is all about prison. One of my colleagues explained how he was in a group that went to Stillwater Prison, interviewed inmates and formulated suggestions about attendance for the new high school in our district. They arrived in the morning, clearing security. Arrangements had been made to interview 30 cooperative offenders (is that an oxymoron?) about high school experiences. The results were initially muddled until they realized the majority of inmates did not graduate at all. Their conclusion: ensure that as many students as possible get a diploma. To achieve that, tough policies were enacted deterring students from missing classes that might compromise their ability to graduate. In a way, we decided to prevent students from ending up in prison *by instituting it* in high school. Thus, the ones who make it now are less likely to land in jail. As for the ones who do not make it, and there are many, well, guess what? We are still 100 per cent tax-receipt responsible for their education — which will be lousy — and together we bear the costs of any later incarceration.

There is a teacher in our building, past her prime. But she does have house and car payments, a son in college and this is no time to be pulling the plug on her hefty salary. A messy divorce has left her bitter; she does not look or sound happy. She's put on weight and her eyes and face have shrunk from the world. When she walks past, only the slightest breeze can be felt. Kids refer to her as the "worksheet lady." And true to form, every day she has her worksheets ready, an assignment on the board. She won't be judged incompetent in her every five year's observation cycle because she does, in fact, come prepared; and besides, the administrator is an old friend. Setting up the task — don't forget attendance! — might take her five minutes; then it is time to work, read, fill in the blank, and most students do it because to get on her bad side is...well...bad news. But she knows who isn't there, who came in tardy and who should be removed for truancy. The prison sentence here is 50 minutes a day, five days a week. The ticket out costs just three classes without an excuse.

What happens in far too many classes such as this is not learning; it is a kind of trivia contest, where information is transferred from book or lecture onto a blank line, and no attempt is made at relationship, common experience or deep understanding. (This is the reason today's students feel no compunction about copying work from others: Does it really matter where a stupid right answer came from?) Paolo Freire, the late Brazilian educational theorist, critiques this traditional method as being based on a "banking" model, where established authorities control the currency, rates of withdrawal, and especially the accounts of customers — in this case, the students. At any time, the authorities can demand, through an exam, that customers account for the information they have been allowed to withdraw. If students can't produce an acceptable account of what has been loaned out, they can be foreclosed upon and eliminated as customers. It works well for producing dull, unimaginative, incapable graduates who lack initiative and critical ability, but it does not cut the mustard for citizens living in a complex democratic society in the 21st century.

A student's final grade in a course should be based on how he or she did on the whole — discussing, writing, producing ideas, mastering material — not a scorecard of how often they came or whether they had permission to be gone. A class involves activities that move students forward; missing it will have its own negative trajectory without resorting to additional administrative head-slapping. Perhaps not every student is mature enough to make responsible choices, but then, when or how will they ever be? A few more cuffs to their self-esteem and GPA? Blindly following what they are told by those in charge? To assume that when the gong sounds on their 18th birthday, kids suddenly become responsible and make good decisions is an absurd child-development fairy tale. (And by the way, do adults always make such great choices?)

We learn from making our own judgments, formulating strategies, feeling real pain and having to go back and get it right. Do young people sometimes need assistance and guidance? Yes. But this is precisely where the job is to help them develop skills to care and plan for themselves, not to stand over them, sword in hand, ready to run them through for the least mistake. There needs to be a larger carrot than a stick for kids to stay in education; more reasons to "stick it out" than "stick it in" the system's ear. Yet, we have created schools where the price of missing a single class —

one class — has gone up and is now enough to eliminate a student from important awards and honors at graduation. That's not education or learning; it's a kind of *fascism*.

In any case, I don't abide the school's attendance policy and have never really had to worry. I mark my bubbles but ignore excused or unexcused and fight administrators wanting to remove kids from my class. Will some of these students become deviant as a result? Will they drop out of life, get addicted, produce unwanted babies? I can't say. But I do know the only proven strategy that prevents these things in the first place is to forge vital relationships between students and adults, and also amongst peers. This is always our best hope and first order of business. The naked fact is: we have established places where children learn and made it mandatory. If kids reject this in large numbers then we need to spend at least half our time looking in the mirror — *à la* Mr. Baker — asking what we are doing wrong. The other half should be dedicated to building prisons, because we will need a lot of them.

* * *

Jenny approaches the podium asking to see the nurse. She is quiet, slightly plump, drinks a ton of soda pop and looks decidedly unwell just now. "What's wrong, Jenny?" In a rare moment of awareness, I remind myself not only to be empathetic but to express it, which I do by raising brows, looking her in the eyes. "My stomach is messed up." I fill in the pink pass required for a nurse visit, change my bubble sheet and tell her I hope she feels better. *This might be just a girl thing*, I think. Just then, Tony walks in, the class clown. He considers himself a ladies' man, though at 5'4" has all the potential of a huggable mascot. He is disheveled, with a pen behind his ear and is stuffing in the last of a blueberry muffin.

"Tony. You're late!" He shrugs. "That's a tardy." He shrugs again.

"Man, I hungry. How can you 'spect me concentrate when my stomach growl all the time." His delivery is hip-hop, involves significantly clipped consonants. He doesn't always look at me but kind of gauges the reaction in his audience. In reality, he's a good-natured kid, he just needs attention — more than I have at this particular moment. I know this because I know Tony; I've taken the time.

"No materials?" Tony mimes a quick search of himself, then pulls the pen out, thrusting it forward. Kids roar; it's a good show, not Elvis, but definitely entertaining. "I'll mark you for no notebook or folder." He swings his arm in disgust. I have no intention of doing this, saying it with a mix of humor and rebuke. This is definitely a guy thing, I think, changing bubbles. "Tony, here today." Then I reconsider. I need to take a tougher stand: he's tardy, has no notebook, is eating in class, his pants are belted mid-thigh and now this small act of rebellion. Part of showing kids you care is not allowing them to wander too far without a concerted "Waz'up, man?" There are boundaries after all… and fences…and holding rooms… and penitentiaries.

"Tony. I want to see you after class." He groans. It's a kind of formality and either or both of us might forget, but it's my standard ploy for settling a kid down, extracting better behavior. (A sanction looms and they want it minimal.) How teachers decide to hold students like Tony accountable — or try to — is something I have wrestled with for years and is so complicated that is brings forth legions of well-paid authors and consultants. A teacher lives and dies a thousand deaths according to policies, when to press them, when to let them go. I can't pretend to get every call right — teaching is more art than science and involves contingencies, not certitudes. I only know that every rule in my arsenal has had to change at one time or another given a particular student or circumstance.

For those taking notes, here is *school life lesson number seven.* The truth is: *you really do need to know what you are doing from the very first minute in a classroom.* A basic question for me is: what will most assist Tony, or any student, to become a better human being? Spending the period in the office waiting for an administrator, clowning with aides? Holding a grudge against me or the school? Or building academic skills, engaged with other students for the next hour? It's genuinely a tough call. Don't misunderstand. I am not an "anything goes" kind of teacher; I have more rules and expectations than most. And like many, I write them up and go over them — on the second day of class. (Day 1 shouldn't be so serious; for my sake, if no one else's.) I even read them aloud, authoritatively, from my handout: "A student's grade will be composed of these three elements: Participation, Written Work and Journals. Students will be asked to sit in groups of three and work constructively on tasks I set before them. Each group will be evaluated every class with a score between 10 and 20. Students also judge their own effectiveness in a group and explain their self-evaluation to peers."

In fact, I have an entire system, exceptionally well-codified. I put kids in groups of three at trapezoidal tables, the room formed into a large horseshoe, allowing me good access at all times. (It's not a circle, but close; everyone sees and hears each other.) Everyday, one group will win the scroll, a colorful Guatemalan fabric wrapped around a piece of parchment, tied with a bolo and a few other emblems acquired over the years. On the parchment, a few words recognize "the exemplary achievements" of this group, in demonstration of the principle that "in this very complex and diverse world, we are all, one people, one village, one world." The group performing most admirably is awarded it; together or individually they get extra credit on anything handed in. (I know this sounds like a small thing, even trite, but you can't believe the importance attached to it as students enter class every day. They really "care" who has it.)

In addition, I have all kinds of specialized regulations to measure student participation — carrots and sticks (soft ones) for helpfulness, determination, absences, off-task behavior, lack of effort, and a myriad of other tricks and procedures that work to keep class running smoothly, respectful. I rarely have to use sticks — kids prefer carrots — but when I do, I do so cheerfully, positively, as much as possible in the good-natured spirit of "This is a great opportunity to learn something." Here is another part of my system. I call it "asset thinking" and contrast it with "deficit thinking" — a negative approach to life that kids readily understand and identify with: there are complainers and people creative enough to see possibilities. According to studies, asset thinkers end up (no surprise) happier, with more friendships, better jobs, and they live longer. We read, discuss and examine what this means, how it's done. We even practice identifying assets at the end of a unit or trimester. Throughout the year, reinforced at illustrative moments, pondered in journal entries, asset thinking becomes part of my student's perceptual framework. (A few students even come to realize that in a basic sense, we create the world we see through our attitude about it.)

For me, my system works. (Knowingly or not, every teacher creates a system.) It's a modified cooperative learning strategy capitalizing on the power of groups to produce useful discussion, reduce tension and increase connections. The concept is not new — I learned about it in my second year of teaching — but the way I have adapted it to my style of teaching is likely unique. I rotate groups frequently — every 10 days — arranging them to promote balance, cooperation and productive encounters. Three is somehow a magic number; more than a pair, less than a committee. You are perpetually one vote from the majority or minority, thus within equal distance of being a champion or bum, a delightful tension. In a short time, using daily group-work, this class becomes a community of learners — integrative, constructive, bonded. Teachers who spend an inordinate amount of time resisting or combating the tendency of students to connect with peers are making an unlimited mistake. Schools need greater connection and integration amongst their diverse clientele, not packs of individuals who don't give a damn about each other.

A typical activity in my class is to have students read a selection from a book. Invariably, we are working within some framework — romanticism, Native spirituality, post-war expansion issues, etc. Together we have formulated insights and notes from readings, investigations, prior knowledge. (I try to minimize my role as keeper of ultimate wisdom, maintaining as high a ceiling as possible for connections because there are always a few students as bright or brighter than myself.) I put a question on the overhead: one of those digging, interpretive kinds, requiring links to previously learned concepts. As a community of learners, this ritual of starting off together is essential. There isn't one right answer, I make that clear, but effective ones link up to what we have already learned, use specific evidence, and provide unusual insight or analysis. These are repeated, scrutinized, celebrated. Early on, I model exemplary essays, and in no time they are after it, making sure theirs fits the framework. Groups rotate through different roles, one person leading the inquiry, another recording an answer, a third responsible for reporting. Discussions are generally excellent because students have rehearsed and want to compete for recognition and reward (remember the scroll!).

Cooperative learning as a means of developing social capital within school is an unbelievable asset: reducing tension and violence, promoting involvement and self-esteem, multiplying connections and interest. ("Meta-studies" on cooperative learning are virtually unanimous about this.) Moreover, it flat out makes for a better experience for everyone, including the over-taxed instructor. When it comes to rules and discipline, nothing is more effective than old-fashioned peer pressure. Groups help to police themselves, knowing that they are linked in terms of performance. For whatever reason — a background in sports, my family circus growing up, a reluctance or even inability to lecture ad nauseum — using groups as teams, cajoling them, building competitive balance, sending them out on challenges, fits my temperament exactly.

As painful and boring as courses can be, it is also true that a positive class culture, once established, can feed and sustain itself a long time, growing into something greater than the sum of its parts. Students learn to welcome contributions and ideas, look forward to discussions, units, groups and challenges. Instead of wanting to miss and skip, they choose to show up and join in. Like everyone, they are happier and more fulfilled being part of something worthwhile, rather than passing on something they consider useless. *Lesson number eight: Adolescents have an unquenchable need to be together, to take pleasure and learn from one another.* The possibility of multiplying this essential need revolutionizes the job of teaching, allowing a teacher to step back from being in their face as authority and truly get to know them as human beings.

* * *

"Today..." I start, and the phone rings. The air comes out of my balloon. "Excuse me." I stride across the room. "Henry. 214." It's the office — they have a habit of calling at the most inopportune times. They want to know if Sara is in class — attendance. She is, I tell them, though I don't mention that she already has her head down. Poor thing is having a rough year. Tall, dishwater blonde, completely out of it, though not without ability. Something about her home life or the lack thereof that I may or may not ever know about. She seems like a good kid — genuine, friendly, courteous, I'll know more by winter break. (Funny, that a system so addicted to accountability does not have a category for "mental truancy"; we require bodies, not minds.) That's all they wanted; I hang up. Tony has found his chair, Nicole is back from the bathroom, and with luck, Jenny will come in at any moment from the nurse.

The game plan is to simultaneously do a dozen things. On the most basic level, the task is to move this group along in terms of skill development — today that means writing. I recently introduced the distinction between skills and knowledge, asking the class which is more vital to their future and why. There was serious head scratching until I took a volunteer to the center to conduct a mock job interview: "When was Abraham Lincoln first elected to the House of Representatives?" "Name 3 signatories to the *Declaration of Independence?*" (Knowledge) "Tell me which of your communication skills you think is most developed and provide examples." "Explain what makes you creative and what you have done with it recently." (Skills) Light bulbs turn on. Knowledge is discreet, can be easily lost or forgotten. Skills are broad, open-ended, and while they may atrophy, essentially endure and are readily transferable.

If you had been in this class since the first week, I would have taken a chunk of time to show you how, because of our changing society, three particular skills have replaced "reading, writing and arithmetic" as the basis of being "well-educated." If nothing else, I insist on a certain level of specificity and structure in ideas so students understand there is real substance behind being called "intelligent" — and also that, ultimately, a big part of being skilled is remembering crucial details.

The first of these new skills is: *Learning how to learn.* It's first because it absolves me from explaining why students have to memorize facts for other classes, like Baker's. They don't in mine because I do not want them wasting time on low-order thinking; though extensive notes — a skill — come in handy on exams where essays require specific evidence. Everyone needs to prove they can learn for a host of reasons, most especially because demographers say we will switch careers at least five times during our work life. Not to mention the raw necessity of getting a post-secondary education. (Lifetime income differentials for secondary versus post-secondary graduates continue to accelerate.) I build into the structure of class a basic but helpful strategy for devising questions and reward students for their use of it. The idea here is that a student must figure out for herself how she learns best — especially what questions to ask — apply it consistently, then continually refine and perfect it. Once she has learned how to learn, other skills and topics, not to mention the rest of life, become more manageable.

The second skill you would have learned is: *Working effectively with others.* This has tremendous intuitive appeal for young people. Earth is full to overflowing with homo sapiens; for better or worse, we are stuck with each other. A few calculated illustrations about how hard it can be — living in a family, getting along with friends — suffice to bring every student along. Repeated conflict, failed relationships and endless bickering are all signs that basic people skills are not adequate. Ones who adapt and enlist others to their cause are more successful, whether at work, in community or raising a family. I allow that there is no better time to start growing that touch with humans than in my class because, as I make clear, students will have to work with everybody in class anyway. By year's end, concerns about relationship skills will be buried beneath a cascade of first-hand experience: joy, camaraderie, cooperation, mutual discovery, and occasional let-downs — vital lessons for everyone.

The last of the "mega-skills" is: *Being a problem solver/critical thinker.* It is, as it suggests, all about being smart, creative and persistent. A critical thinker can identify the crux of a problem and propose ways to attack it. Managers do not want employees who run to them with every minor difficulty or unexpected challenge because their brain is inflexible or dull. Neither do we want citizens who can't trouble-shoot their way past a skilled telemarketer. Whether it is called "street smarts," "quick on your feet" or just "common sense," all of us need to work out solutions for life's little conundrums. Something doesn't add up? A cell-phone bill inflated? The hog farm smell? Sit down, focus, and figure out what it is, how it can be handled. In the Information Age, if you can't successfully navigate information, sort the helpful from the useless and propose a way through it, you may as well strap on a life-vest because you are destined to drown.

Crucial educational truth number nine: Teaching kids to build skills, not just knowledge, is essential in education. We should not waste time requiring memorization of useless information or facts. Nor does filling in a blank with answers gleaned from a textbook constitute important skill development. Education should be much more about "applying" knowledge to resolve questions and issues, creating new knowledge, which is, after all, a skill. By using cooperative groups, students are continuously growing people skills without consciousness of it happening. Unfortunately, trying to stimulate and evaluate other skill development is tricky, time-consuming and labor intensive. In English, it dooms the instructor to endless reading, whether papers or journals or exams, and to evaluation of presentations, research skill and interpersonal abilities.

A commitment to thorough evaluation with feedback for 150 students a day is within the quality circle established by Mother Theresa. Just 10 minutes a week talking with or evaluating the work of each student outside of class adds up to 25 hours of intensive, highly focused work. What about other professional responsibilities? Teaching class, planning, organizing special events such as speakers, field trips or projects? The need to stay current, contact parents, consult colleagues, respond to e-mail and handle administrative reporting like grades? Not to mention your family and spouse and the rest of your life, which is supposed to be there to keep you sane. *Undeniable truth number ten: If you are a determined teacher, no matter how air-tight your system or your level of experience, you are in way over your head.*

* * *

What I have detailed so far comes reasonably close to what happens in my class. But it only approximates the job's complexity, and especially the spontaneous give and take with kids, which is its bread and butter. I haven't mentioned curriculum yet, including how important it is for a teacher to not just know it, but know how to deliver it en masse. (Remember? It's about relationship and transfer. Will you bore them?

Confuse them? Go too slow or fast?) The ability to speak clearly, effectively plan short- and long-term, and design engrossing lessons integrating new material are all important. You also need to monitor progress so you can adjust accordingly. (Listen to students; look at their faces. Are they with you? Do we need to review, re-teach, revisit anything?) Then also realize that this whole enterprise will go down the toilet quickly if you cannot be balanced and fair handling grades. You are still a representative of established authority. And when the shit hits the fan, whether a fight or other problem beyond your control, you cannot shirk responsibility as the adult, the one appointed to be fair and reasonable. Remember: students watch and learn from everything you do. A teachable moment comes around only a hundred times a day.

And even if a teacher does all of this skillfully, he or she could still fall short of the mark. Short because the job is not just efficiency or versatility or know-how. It may be that *the most important aspect of teaching is to inspire youngsters*; to fill them with hope, desire, and curiosity to become someone extraordinary. ("Life, oh life!" according to Whitman.) This is the *sine qua non* of education and *point number 11* on this thumb-nail tour of high school. How to accomplish it is elusive. It isn't just unusual talent or high achievement. It isn't just being friendly or kind. It isn't just extra help or important feedback. It isn't just about being unique, bizarre, edgy, or non-conforming. In fact, it is all of these things and more — much more — delivered in the right amount, at precisely opportune moments.

When a child becomes inspired, they will do for themselves much more than anyone can do for them; once lit, the lamp of scholarship infuses a life-long burning to learn. How to inspire a young person is mysterious and intangible but happily, not entirely rare. Who cares if a teacher can decipher Shakespearean sonnets, memorize the periodic table or sing arpeggios in Italian? Can they awaken in students a desire to do something similar? Teaching doesn't mean being a fountain of knowledge as much as creating a fountain in your room: one with an inviting pool that attracts students to sit around, wade out, and, loosening all sense of self-consciousness, revel in the deepest, most invigorating places. The job is to get them immersed in their own process — thinking, relating, imagining, connecting, creating — so they become a well-spring for making their own meaning.

* * *

Teachers are doomed to fail with at least some of the many qualities expected of them; many teachers fail in multiple ways, yet are wildly successful at others. We fail all the time; every day. We have to. The job, as described above, is unmanageable: 150 students a day; 170 days a year. You, your system, and the clock. Try to accomplish as much as possible. Unfortunately, it will never be enough to make everyone happy. We're 5 minutes into class and there is nothing approaching magic yet. Shrug. I understand how listlessness can become the norm, not only amongst kids but also for the teacher. As colleagues, we share only one essential mission: to take this unpolished group and promote them to their next class and year and teacher. To funnel them toward the other end, where Mark, Lakeisha and Amy are now — as countless before them — hoping that, with a carefully considered leap or a clumsy uninspired lurch, they transition to college or work or a life beyond. It is, in all truth, their own responsibility.

The consequences of a poor education crash down on the backs of students, their family and community, never on the school or teacher. That is why it is so incredibly easy to under-perform as an educator. It is also why pundits and politicians have been so successful in controlling debate with their "standards" agenda. Test scores provide the illusion of success or failure, a measured result which can be held up to scrutiny, debate and repercussion. Finally, schools and teachers can be held accountable for not succeeding at their impossible job "Here is the proof!" And yet, in either case, success or failure, what is being called for with standards is just more of the same tired pedagogy and curriculum that never worked in the first place. Accountability through uniform testing is not an answer for educational shortcomings; it is part and parcel of an approach that limits student interest in the first place. The fact that a certain wager of tax money is tied to each student's neck or that a politician has been elected on reform will never be enough to make learning valuable or inspired. For better or worse, that's up to the human beings whose job it is to be with children day-in, day-out, whose task it is to love impossible work and each child as their own.

We are nearing the end of this whirlwind tour. I've tried to keep it short and sweet — I have left out a lot — but the world of schooling is dense. As during a long day going over an explanation for the fifth time, I am afraid I forgot something or misrepresented material. So let's review: Kids have a natural exuberance and desire to interact with their world. For reasons that serve adults, today's schooling frequently employs traditional methods that manage to choke the wonder from them. All teaching is about love, relationship and transfer, not just of data or facts but attitudes, values, compassion, and everything we communicate while not so subtly letting kids know we control their daily lives. If you want to work here, you better know what to do from the very first moment. Make the need and desire for connection amongst adolescents serve the larger program of learning and skill development. Even when you are highly effective, there is no escaping how unmanageable this job really is. So do your best, and just inspire; inspire as many as you can.

If you are a person who wants schools to change and are looking for an agenda to push at the local level, it's this simple: insist upon the best and brightest, most sensible and sensitive people to work with your children. Pay them well. Then train, grow and support them in a humane way, fashioning a system that allows for creativity, personal development and connection as human beings — things you would want for your own kids. In fact: these stressed-out school teachers, from the best to the worst that you and I love to carp about and criticize, *were our own children* at one point. That's why I insist again we must understand a crucial point: We are all students; we are all teachers.

One more thing. If someone makes an argument for or against any proposal, program or initiative based upon increasing or declining test scores, politely tell them to sit down because they don't know what they are talking about. Ask them if they have read the actual books or studies that are out there on this issue. Ask them if they can specifically recall the score on any standardized exam that they have taken in their life, or even a single question or answer from that exam. Ask them how it is that a standardized exam will inspire young learners, or teachers, to create or achieve things that we have yet to even imagine. Or simply inquire when was the last time they spent as much as five minutes — like you have — in a public school.

* * *

I will not resolve this, or even experience wild success on a day like today in Sophomore English. There will be time again tomorrow, next month, even next year. Today is only a small piece, some time practicing a writing technique, further development of Romanticism, introducing Thoreau's *Walden*. There probably will not be anything here today that will change a student's life, but I know in my heart that I must proceed as if there is. And sometimes, by luck or accident or magic, I am surprised.

For example, a couple of years ago, I had a temperamental but creative young woman, small, wiry, headstrong, who frustrated me to wit's end —

leaving class when she felt like it, ignoring key projects, refusing to join discussions. She explained to peers in her final presentation how Thoreau's words, the very ones we will read today, hit their mark: "...if one advances confidently in the direction of his dreams, and endeavors to live the life which he has imagined, he will meet with a success unexpected in common hours." Shauna loved poetry, frequently writing it while the rest of us labored after understanding about a writer, a concept, a movement. She also stuffed my Free Speech Box with entries, would run up from the back when it was time to pull one out and share it with the class. I loved her and hated her because she lived totally on impulse, refusing to bend her will in the least for the needs of others. She warmed my heart on that last day, telling us how important dreams are, how convinced she was that if each one of us follows our heart, we will, like Thoreau, "suck the marrow out of life."

Unfortunately for Shauna, though she fought her way back into class the next year after not registering for it — my final comments on her portfolio pissed her off — I noticed that she was changing as the year sagged to its conclusion. On the final day, one year after telling us to suck marrow, she dropped a bombshell: she was with child and would not be in school for her final year. But she also wished us the happiness of pursuing our dreams and not to follow her poor example, because her life was pretty much limited now, at least for the foreseeable future. She cried and laughed and thanked us all for the experience which, to me, had seemed to barely scratch her tumultuous personality. Heading back to her chair, I thought to myself how much she had changed, become more amenable and contingent to relationship. It wasn't just about herself anymore; other people mattered, especially the one growing inside. Life, or at least high school, had passed her by and was now beating her door down demanding to get back in. We passed around the Kleenex I keep on my desk. Teaching with heart means, periodically at least, being willing to see it torn from your chest and left bloody on the floor.

* * *

"Ladies and gentlemen, my apologies for the unfortunate delay this morning. Like everything in life there is only so much you control. I would like to remind you: tardies do accumulate and have a deleterious impact on your participation grade." Tony's eyebrows are raised; he looks around mouthing "deleterious?" I love parts of this job. "I ask you to consider carefully, as I did, the comments that appear on your efforts from yesterday. If you need elaboration or have questions, please speak with me individually. Right now, I would like everyone to please take out a sheet of paper. Jake, this means you." Jake is one of the better prepared students and my occasional whipping boy to cue others. He is already calmly looking ahead with paper and pen in hand, having read the board where class activities are listed. I maneuver the overhead projector, pull out the transparency that I know works for this purpose — writing to show and not tell. Basically teaching to write with specific details, not generalities. I have a crummy, general paragraph; they spice it up, make it come alive, then read these to each other before we take volunteers.

It'll do for this part of class, maybe 15 minutes. Keep it moving. Lots of action and activities; allow groups to do the work of building skills and relationships. I look out and detect major glazing and unconnectedness. It has been a rough start; so many delays and interruptions. "Let's go back first." I tell them. Even I make mistakes. (Get them warmed up, you dummy!) "Before we create something the world has never seen — ever; who can tell me what happened yesterday?" I need to take some time to knit together yesterday and today, create a continuous fabric from this chopped-up mess we call a school day. I set groups discussing and, by God, they do it. Many years ago it surprised me, but not anymore. I expect it; I insist on it. The classroom teacher has the biggest impact on a student's education. Be damned good, I remind.

Lori raises first: "We did a practice writing and you gave us a writing assignment." I ask what it was about. She pauses, I call on Tom. "We have to research and like, become foreigners who go to America." I look confused: "Foreigners?" "Immigrants." Lori pounds home vindicated. Sarah is starting to sit up with her chin in her hand, determined not to crumble. We nail down another five or six things that occurred yesterday. A compact mirror gets folded up. I even call on one of the Heavy Chevy boys, Mark, who is able to produce the obscure fact that anyone not giving one of the required speeches will not graduate under new Minnesota rules. Funny the things kids remember. I'm in my body now, moving in front of class. If skills and collaboration are your fundamental message, you can't stand monolithically behind the podium like a statue of knowledge. You have to move, enjoy the dance, embody skillfulness yourself.

"On the sheet of paper, I want you to draw yourself in the upper-right-hand corner instead of writing your name. Now, the deal is, you have to include some telling detail which any reasonable person could identify. Let me repeat this…" I flip on the overhead and mock up an image of myself, ponytail and goatee being the key elements. (Model your tasks. Always model.) I sound like a circus barker working the crowd before a show. Heads bend to the task, many of them pondering what makes them unique, vaguely unsure what I will do with their image, some swearing they can't draw. Jenny strides in from the nurse. Tony turns to a kid for paper and pulls the pen theatrically from his ear: Zorro ready for a duel.

After a bit, I launch the writing practice. "Why do we do practice writings?" No one moves. Finally, after an appropriate amount of thinking, I call on Allen, a reserved kid, at least in this class, who likes basketball but has no particular future in it: "Because if you want to be good at something; you need to practice." He's there. A girl, Leah, follows out: "It's a skill. And that's what we're going to need for our jobs is skills" She's pretty much there. "Why skills? What's so great about skills?" We are off and running. Amongst all the other things I mentioned about teaching, I almost forgot an important one; one that makes this little march through high school cleaner now because we have finally arrived at a full dozen: *Above all, an effective teacher has to sell.* Sell as many as 150 teenagers on the present — and their future — every single day.

bad days and sleepless nights

I didn't know it at the time, but I made it as a teacher when the G-people showed up in my room after school. It was more than a month past September 11th and they were apparently breaking-in new agents. "Mr. Henry, we are with the F.B.I." A brusque and professional woman delivered the punch-line. "We are here to arrest you." My jaw dropped; I must have looked sad and confused; I was having a week. She was only joking, looking for that fun ice-breaker into a difficult thing, but it went lost on me — their job and mine at that point anything but fun.

Sour events had begun with Sandy in my classroom after a newspaper meeting on Monday. She was a squat girl, African-American, more pyramid than hour glass. Her hair was a nest pushed off to one side; she had fierce brown eyes and a long masculine cut to her jaw. Her voice was hollow, retreating, coming from back in her throat in an artificially high-tone, as if purposely formed to sound like she thought a girl's should. Shy, coy, she started by expressing doubts about her assignment: writing a story about the newly arrived sophomore class. What to write about? She slowly worked to other topics: "Mr. Henry, you don't really know me that well, do you? I'm not like most girls. What if, Mr. Henry, what if I told you something about myself that makes me really different? I mean, I am different you know. I don't live with my mommy and daddy." Her eyes bounced the floor to my face. Hemming, hawing, she spilled her truth: not only was she in a foster program, she had a two-year-old daughter at age 16.

It took a few more newspaper meetings and some time with the social worker, but eventually details surfaced. Sandy had been raped by her mother's boyfriend in Tennessee, and even though her mother still lived with the man, the best efforts of local authorities could not produce either a responsible father or the callous perpetrator. The depravity of her story, the innocent strength of her willingness to be a mom, a student, a foster child, a rape victim and also a news reporter clawed its way into my spirit as hope but also weighed down my other duties as teacher. Hideous crimes even far away have a way of leaving scars.

That's how the week started. It would end on Friday with Christina, one of my best students, being forcibly and legally removed from school by her father who lived in Illinois. It was a parental-custody dispute. He wasn't a bad person; in fact, he was a minister near Chicago, but when he heard that his daughter was living with an aunt — and not with her mother who had moved out of our district — he exploded at the deception. Christina was a natural leader, organizing charity basketball for the Heart Association, joining organizations, standing for election. She also was wonderful in class, sharing genuine thoughts, ideas, feelings, lifting peers to a higher level. This was my second year of working with her; I had seen her laugh and cry, love and scold, but always wanting something important and strong and beautiful to come from her efforts. She was an open spirit determined to make a difference; now she was just gone. No goodbyes, no closure. Her father came at 1:55 and by 2:15, papers were signed and she was headed to Illinois with just the clothes on her back.

In between Sandy and Christina was Sara and the F.B.I. She was in the same class as Christina, an excellent writer and bright. The previous year, she had given me a touching card on the last day thanking me for improving her writing. She told me it was the first anyone had cared that much about her. For the last few weeks I had detected something odd: she seemed distracted, aloof, uninterested. Sara sat blankly in class and, even though she had excellent rapport with others, barely engaged. Mostly, she just wrote intensely in her journal as class moved along. We had a major writing assignment due that week: a narrative about some key event in the life of our family. Apparently this had sparked her, particularly after she asked me, weeks prior, if she could modify the assignment. She wanted to write about an incident that summer on a mission trip in Montana. I was hesitant, but acceded to it, sensing that this was terribly more important than I might realize. A call from her mother and now this visit from the F.B.I. confirmed suspicions: Sara had been sexually assaulted during her mission trip and because it happened on a federal reservation, the F.B.I. had the case. They wanted to read her paper, lift it from my file and enter it as evidence. I felt somewhat gratified that an outside authority had validated the importance of student portfolios, but I limped home deflated that weekend, my sense of professional efficacy having taken another blow.

* * *

For the longest time, I believed I had a special affinity for teaching girls. As a youngster, whenever the issue of gender inequities or male sexism surfaced, I beat a hasty retreat behind having five older sisters and generated instant credibility for being liberated. And if being compelled to vacuum, do dishes, make my bed or face getting pinned to the floor with a tangle of icky hair in my face was the price of liberation, I would gladly pay it again. The fact is, I knew better than to put limits on what girls could do: I saw them practicing instruments, studying for exams, playing softball, reading books, shoveling the walk. They were smarter, stronger, more talented and definitely more skilled at putting me in a verbal head-lock where the only way out was crying "Uncle."

I never gave an ounce of consideration as to how this might translate into a profession like teaching. Mostly, as I describe elsewhere, I was a novice educator full of my own concerns, fears and inadequacies. Yet, despite a rough first year in which students — especially girls — felt perfectly at home walking all over me, I came to believe that I was particularly effective teaching young women. In an odd way, this was not my fault. In the late '80s and early '90s, studies were coming out, even whole books (Carol Gilligan comes to mind) about how girls were being substantially short-changed at school, particularly in advanced classes and grade levels. The studies indicated that a majority suffered from low self-esteem; that whereas boys were confident and received attention, girls languished holding all the right answers inside. To control preternaturally more rambunctious boys, teachers called on them repeatedly, ignoring well-behaved young women. As in my family, the squeaky wheel got the oil.

All of this made sense and sounded valid enough that I set about observing and correcting deficiencies. Over a matter of months, even years, I came to the conclusion that I was a ground-breaking instructor. In my classes, girls were invariably the best students, participated extremely well, did more conscientious work at home and on projects, helped others and generally followed through. I convinced myself that by using group work, emphasizing relationships — and because of all my older sisters — girls flourished in my class environment. They were the ones I most enjoyed, who took time to establish a relationship, and it gave me particular pride to know I was bucking a national trend.

As the '90s rolled along, it became more and more apparent that there were significant gender issues in education, but not what we had been led to believe. As it happens, young men, and at times elementary boys, showed up at school with guns and killed classmates, teachers, principals — first in Arkansas, then Kentucky, Oregon, Florida, Pennsylvania, and of course, eventually, most spectacularly, in Colombine, Colorado. Researchers rushed to fill the knowledge gap: girls might be doubting themselves in school but they weren't willing to murder for it. Drop-out rates for boys increased; teenage pregnancies for girls declined. New studies emerged that pointed out that girls academically out-perform boys, on balance feel better about school, develop more meaningful relationships, are more involved, and by almost every measure are more successful, except in advanced math and science courses. By decade's end, virtually every precept about how girls are short-changed in school had been challenged; the spot-light now fell on how we failed at boys. I nodded: I sure had a lot of underperformers in my courses — guys that just sat and never did much, refusing to emote or even emit at all.

Like many teachers, I went from unusually successful to mostly average without changing a thing. What had changed was not even the world around me, but rather our perception of it; at least as unsystematically ruled by some nameless, faceless elite whose job it is to generate ideas about education. Girls weren't the problem, it was boys headed down the toilet and no one could really say why.

Every year, more studies come out, more trends to discuss, further points of national emphasis — declining test scores, modified standards, rating schools. Old timers tell me that if I stick around long enough, I'll get to see each trend at least three times — each promising to revolutionize education. The really big cynics sit in the back during teacher workshops and don't do much because they have seen fads and fixes blow through and land in the dumpster as quickly as they arrive. Somehow, those underperforming boys in my classes have all ended up at the back of faculty meetings as veteran public school teachers.

* * *

A teacher's most basic task is to ask questions and evaluate answers: put a frame around material or concepts and compel young minds to encounter it. As I have tried to show, that seemingly simple process involves so many complicating factors — outside demands, pedagogical issues, submerged psychological debris — that it often takes a backseat to the "real" basics: the ones that come and sit at desks. Despite that, especially in high school, there comes a time when ideas, concepts, perhaps even a philosophy of living, however hazy, begins to form itself. The child makes a move toward becoming adult. Family plays a large role in early development, friends have their outsized influence during adolescence, then if we are lucky, teachers or at least some gleaming subject, field or pursuit pulls or pushes them toward a bigger life. Finding that third leg, merging a sense of self into notions of how the world works is tricky, existential, even at times accidental. It is also crucial. A good teacher has a first opportunity to invite students into this beyond where wisdom, scholarship and clashing ideas yoke their particularized existence to a larger chain. Hopefully, they see that what is framed in those questions includes themselves, or at least that there is a role to play shedding light and making deposits in the storehouse of knowledge.

The most significant aspect of this process as I see it, is to encourage students to confront their own curiosity and profound uncertainties. To ask them what concerns they have — what hopes, fears, dreams, visions and questions. Not so they can come up with some final answer or see facts and ideas as an ultimate solution, but rather, so they connect their inner world — -their personal place of spirit — with some larger realm. It's that connection between an outer world of issues, ideas and theory with an inner world of wonder, doubt and perplexity which convinces a person that learning is valuable, that being in school presents opportunities to grow, be creative and become wise. What is needed is a spark that jumps across the gulf of separation from their internally saturated sense of identity to the exterior — people, ideas and objects worthy of collaboration.

* * *

I had my one big week after my one big decade on the issue of girls and education. No, I am not uniquely talented at teaching them, and they aren't being short-changed at school: *it's our culture that wants to eat them alive*. The F.B.I. got Sara's paper but never found a suspect, just as Sandy's "baby-daddy" still rules a roost somewhere down south. After a few months and some gentle prodding, we got Christina back to finish her junior year. As for the guys, they both hold their own and don't change much at all. "Boys will be boys" means teachers are forever on-guard for the clever and feckless while hunching their shoulders over ones that never wake up.

I wonder sometimes about the issues we create from reading and thinking and proposing distinctions between groups or genders or classes in school. There are important insights to be gained but also dangerous conclusions drawn. Where the mind can't find a clean answer or sure logic, one will be created that fits neatly for the data. There is always a right answer. And now because of testing, there is unlimited data, and thus unlimited analysis of what we need to do to get every child to produce the exact same answer to all our questions. If you listen too much to experts or prevailing opinion, you might convince yourself that you are better or worse, more or less than others, when what really matters most — like so much of life — is simply to be yourself: to be alert, sensitive and reflect upon what you see happening around you.

This is what is meant by the term being a "reflective" teacher: someone who has the patience and aptitude to sit down at night and ruminate about what they have seen. They have an unlimited drive to find ways to do better. Too much happens during a school day for a teacher to handle each experience with consummate humanity and skillfulness at the moment it occurs. But there is usually another chance and the best take advantage to ponder their next move, a strategy for penetrating a young student's defenses or recapturing a wayward class. A few even stay up at night unable to sleep until something useful comes. They shift and turn, their job at the surface and a mind busily trying to work it out. In between taking the pulse of their own circumstance, they occasionally venture a finger to the wind, wondering if there isn't a better way we could all be doing this.

play

The greatest catch I ever saw came in the top of the eighth inning with two runners on in a tie game. The Yankees were in town, Mickey Mantle was the batter, and my brother Steve was pitching. He chewed gum nervously. An oily Twins hat held down curly hair and, because it was a hot afternoon and he was throwing hard, perspiration pooled in spots on his T-shirt. The atmosphere grew tense as he stared in, paused — the announcer building this up — then whipped the ball against the steps. There was a solid smack; it flew high and deep. Steve, also playing outfield and doing the live broadcast, ran to the wall — in this case our lilac bushes — leapt high, thrusting his arm and torso into the branches and near as I could tell... probably made the catch. The play-by-play cut off, but he got up, tennis ball in glove and finished the double-play running back to the mound. A remarkable moment. Steve's version of the crowd — this shushing-rumbling growl done deep-throat — went wild. Even I clapped from my seat under the overhang. He retrieved his hat, then went on to shut-out the Yankees while the Twin's Tony Oliva, catching a pitch on the perfect edge of the third step, sent one clear to the alley in the tenth.

It wasn't unusual to see Major League ball played out against our backsteps, nor to have Tom Dempsey or George Blanda kick winning field goals over our clothes-line from a coffee can in a driving snow. Every kind of play was welcome and inevitable. With nine children on staff, we didn't need neighbors, though we included them for variety and to distribute pain more equitably. Our house occupied a corner lot and we scheduled events with precision. If baseball diamonds were in use, kickball out front. If rinks were full, snow football in the side yard. We were minutes from a wading pool, merry-go-round, swings, a teeter-totter, monkey bars and tether-ball; if all else failed, there was always two, three, or four square, the sandbox, a walk to the Little Store or a ride on our bikes. When it rained, we went downstairs, rearranged furniture, killed the lights and played *Alligator*. Or turned them on and played *Simon Says, Hopscotch, Jacks, Marbles, Twister*, or got down one of the zillion board games — *Hands Down, Clue, Monopoly* — or played a half-dozen different card games. Or got sick of it all and just made crank phone calls.

Sports, or anything involving competition predominated, but at times there was no game; it was play in pure form — for the fun of it. The alley behind our house had a gentle slope, and snow, when melting, ran down to a low spot where it spilled onto 9th street. In Spring, or after a good rain, damming became a fascination. (Yes, a boy thing.) We had engineers, inspectors, suppliers and workers organized into a single operation by the personnel director, my brother Mike. We held water back with mud, ice and cardboard (whatever was in the trash), then formed sluiceways below the dam, leaving objects worthy of disaster — toy trucks, margarine tubs, plastic men — in its wake. If a car came, we stood aside, made reluctant waves, then scrambled into "Red alert", rushing back to repair the breaches.

Minnesota winters may seem a blow to a life of play — it definitely froze the alley — but it never phased the Henry's. Not these kids; not me anyway. Winter meant high gear, not a throttle back. There were sliding hills at Hester Park or Mount Calvary, but those we could only get to by convincing our father to take us. We made snowmen and angels, concealed forts within shovel piles and invented secret iconography in drifts with shaky yellow lines. In the back we created tunnels, icing inner walls for security, the yard light at night our only clue as to where and who we really were. We hitched cars, latching onto bumpers in a squat position, seeing how far we got before spinning out or hitting a pavement patch. There were regular snowball fights, sometimes involving the whole block — caches of pre-formed ammo fueling blitzkriegs complete with garbage can lids for the infantry. And of course, there was 'beaning' cars. We had the perfect fence for it: a four-foot basket-weave that older boys could stand behind and throw over like original Greek ramparts. How exciting, the "Thump-Thump-Thump" on a car, like —"Contact has been made with another world!" We never got caught, but then again, winter traffic on 9th Street dropped off quite a bit over the years.

There is no end to stories about play and it's not something I should apologize for, but I sense that someone reading right now is wondering if we aren't a little off-topic here. In all honesty, I don't believe so. In fact, if the subject of this book is school and teaching and learning, we have never been so close to the heart of it. And if the deeper question is identity or growing up or America, this still sails through the essential core. I have a thesis here. That is, in the distant future when we look back and analyze important developments of last century, eclipsing virtually everything will be the under-appreciated contribution of play. That what we have essentially created in America, especially over the last 50 years, is a vast living out of Sigmund Freud's central premise: "[Our] entire psychical activity *is bent upon procuring pleasure* and avoiding pain."

I understand that play has been a human refuge for millennia from China to Africa to Meso-America, but it seems to me that our modern determination for it has been sharpened by an historic increase in leisure time. A close examination of Western civilization reveals how important leisure time has been as a driver of economic trends, social forces, technology, even historical events — from our relatively recent appreciation of food in every variety, to travel and transportation and the reasons for it, to a swift take-over of the economy by the service industry. The emergence of entertainment as an individually consumable pursuit — movies, music, television, theatre, professional sports — and all forms of passionate study and learning, which after all must please the mind if nothing else, have allowed millions to get in on the act, even when they are sitting alone at home. More than ever, there is tremendous choice about what we do and how we do it; guiding that is the determination that it add up to a large measure of fun.

I don't want to beat a dead horse here (though even that could be considered a shabby form of play), but so much modern technology is dictated by our desire/love for play. Cell phones allow instant interplay with another person, anywhere, anytime. Sport utility vehicles haul a ton of toys, suggest a person who knows how (and is rich enough) to play, and are perceived as safer, more likely to keep you alive for later, more precious forms of play. Casinos, which sprang from nowhere to a multi-billion dollar industry in just two decades, are so committed to play that contact with the outside world — like windows — is forbidden. And computers? Mega-play. The electronic games, email, on-line messaging and Web-pages, all variations on the concept of play. And who are the most sophisticated — and dangerous — users of this new medium except so-called "hackers", ones who grew a compulsion through endless on-line play.

Traditional outings — hunting, camping, hiking — according to numbers, have never been more popular. Rock-climbing, mountain biking, snow boarding, parasailing, hang gliding, kayaking, Ultimate Frisbee (to name just a few) and even illicit adventures like spelunking sewers and tunnels or jumping off skyscrapers (with parachutes) are examples of intense play that have recently blossomed into fashion. Extreme sports, reality television, comedy clubs, museums, travel tours of every stripe and flavor, elder-hostels — the list goes on like the games of my youth. Everywhere you look, from the orientation of magazines to the changing meaning of holidays, from word-play in newspaper headlines to jungle gyms at hamburger franchises, play emerges as a dominating presence.

Isn't corporate globalization-through fast-food, Hollywood entertainment, and fun but mostly superfluous products really driven by an American ethos of exporting our individualistic and materialistic culture to the world? And aren't "individualism" and "materialism" the twin towers of modern play that so conflict with traditional societies that Islamic terrorists hope to destroy them before their own culture gets infected?

And consider sports themselves. Most everyone agrees that 'official' play has never been taken to such a level, not only amongst professionals, where salaries, endorsements and new stadiums have mushroomed to absurdity, but also in an individual sense, where personal trainers, nutritional supplements, even performance enhancing drugs have extended competition to the molecular level. And it continues to breach boundaries at every level: children being exhorted on and argued about by overzealous parents; schools and universities compelled to walk the financial plank to produce winning teams; women and girls, who when I was growing up had just a tiny sliver of the opportunities they do today, are now equally enmeshed and enthralled as men and boys. Mainstream clothing and gear is filled with official logos, player jerseys and starter jackets. And contemporary heroes are overwhelmingly entertainers and sports figures when a few decades earlier they were more likely scientists, artists, generals or politicians.

The extent of this topic astonishes me. Every time I reach for its essential implications — I think I have it blocked or controlled — play breaks free, continues downfield and puts me in mind of that alley filling with melt-water behind our amateurish fortifications. Even towards 50, my typical week is a cavalcade of sports and exercise, gatherings, concerts, card games, reading and savoring time with my wife. The best part of teaching is about spontaneity, playing verbally with students or ideas in front of the class. Writing, too, is largely play — hour upon unconscious hour exploring narrative, rooting out *le mot juste*, leading images onto the stage, then circling them back to their proper cages. It's almost like an irascible youth has escaped here, ignoring calls for duty and discipline, refusing to come in and get changed for dinner. I am supposed to be getting older, more settled and sedentary, but play remains my subtle master. It looks in at me from out-of-doors as the promise of nature, and, as my eyes narrow down, is found spying me in the window's soft reflection — like what we are really doing, my likeness and I, is playing *hide-and-go-seek*. The most active of boys has become a man but his essential instincts haven't changed much at all.

* * *

One long-term, pervasive change in attitude of young people which I observed as a teacher is the contemporary determination to be "rich." This value continues to grow in popularity every year. Students stand in front of peers declaring that their main goal in life is to have "a lot of money", the sooner the better. This disheartens me, a sign that consumer impulses have broken in the door, are making off with the most idealistic amongst us: our kids. I cling though to a shred of optimism that this is more about play than anything. That it is a pursuit of human passion and pleasure these kids seek, which, as far as they can tell, only money guarantees them. (Where did they learn that?) The more money you have, the more surely you control the terms and conditions in pursuit of pleasure. They, like me, have been raised on an unending diet of play. Our respective ingredients for it were different though: this may explain why wanting to be rich seemed like a fundamentally off-key idea to young people of my generation. "Why?" We would have asked. "The rich don't have as much fun as we do."

Contemporary teachers are caught up in this national epidemic. (No, they aren't so dumb as to think *they* will be rich.) Play, when stacked up against the needs of a productive, efficient society can appear to be merely self-indulgent, frivolous. Responsible adults seem to be saying: "You kids have it too easy. We're going to enforce a certain script here, at least in your school experience." Perhaps they are jealous of the greater access to play amongst youngsters and are using a generational prerogative to slap them in line. (It wouldn't be the first time that has happened.) Teachers work in a world that expects, desires and treasures having fun, but which is asking that children be put in a metaphorical prison, bars raising on all sides, not invited to see passion and joy — the play — in learning but increasingly, right and wrong answers, tests that prove they are normal enough to advance to the next level of drudgery. And equally troubling, some teachers capitulate so completely to students' need for fun — filling classes with continuous videos, free time, candy, trips to the media center or computer lab and very little effort at generating deeper "fun" — that the standards movement has made serious in-roads with calls for "accountability." Perceptions of "wasteful" play have led directly to initiatives seeking to abolish it altogether.

It is a truism to assert that a happy medium must be found in every teacher's repertoire on the issue of play. On one side is the steep ledge of a class being too stiff, too tight-roped so there is little freedom, natural give-and-take or a sense of spontaneous experience: everyone minding their steps. On the other is the sheer drop-off into jocularity, fun without end, leading to its own kind of dismissal and irrelevancy, as in "This class is a joke." There needs to be middle ground. Children desire fun, and over the long haul, teachers do too, if only to show students what serious play looks like: how it is not about being passive, spending money or going someplace new — except in your mind.

I am not entirely sure how to explain the happy medium except to agree with Parker Palmer that it emerges from the personal character of teachers themselves, their "inner landscape": shaped by family, childhood, years of school, dozens of relationships, and reams of intangibles. And most important, that this process of personal growth and development is continuous; it never ends. As Paulo Freire, the great Brazilian educational theorist suggests, the teacher needs to forge ahead as the most determined of learners, making it clear that they themselves are still experiencing organic progression — are not yet finished — and willing to invest a maximum of energy and interest in each class, every student. The greatest lesson of a good teacher is that there is always more to reap as each moment unfolds — life's contingencies mixing freely with her profound truths — and that this, more than anything, is what establishes our humanity.

In my experience, play is an essential method for capturing imagination and interest in students, especially using structured interaction. I create small groups as teams and use both cooperation and rivalry to instill a sense of involvement and competition. It is framed with an overlay of deep topics and honest discussion — I make it clear that it is *their* class, *their* discoveries that matter most — but I also model good humor so they can forget about being too serious. In this sense, play has no need to divorce itself from hard work or to be banished from the classroom.

My best results have come when I approach kids more in terms of coaching than teaching. My voice sails in over the top as they busily work together, trying to set their team or project on a better course, challenging assumptions, asking them to incorporate skills we have worked on. Learning requires dedication and practice as a sport does, along with patience, perseverance and a kind of respect for the game. And members of a class grow in the same measure as a team does, challenging, helping and teaching each other on a daily basis. I regularly ask them to address where they find themselves vis-à-vis goals, limitations, curiosities; how the material has affected them intellectually, emotionally. Because they each spend time together in groups, this processing is granted high value, real class time. By allowing for every student's experience and insight, giving them a chance to speak their truth in front of everyone, a real "team" emerges — one that is better thought of as a learning community. We have ups and downs, good days and bad, plenty that no one expected. But it is something accomplished together, and by the end of the year, every student has touched someone and contributed no matter their level of overall achievement.

The more intense and "real" this gets, the more fully it rolls up kids in its path. On the last day when we put notes on each other's backs — literally writing on each other's backs in long lines — sharing fond farewells and friendly teasing, there are heartfelt exchanges, genuine expressions that mark the passage on an almost ritualistic level. A class needs emotional intensity and authenticity in order to feel compelling; this is what captures youngsters most completely, attracted as they are to being part of each other's world. This happens largely without fuss or pre-occupation when it comes naturally: students work hard, expend effort but feel no real burden or discomfort. Minds are being flexed, intellectual abilities given a workout. Honesty, generosity, and caring are held up as part of a worthy ethic. As on a field or court in the middle of dynamic play, what they are doing feels right for who they are, for being part of a communally gratifying pursuit.

* * *

Recently, the space ship *Columbia* broke up over the southwest United States and disintegrated, dropping debris and human remains over a wide area. It was an incredible visual sight and indeed a tragedy, nothing like fun or play for anyone; nor is the task (mostly) of determining what went wrong, how to prevent it in the future. What struck and interested me was listening to the biographies of its crew. Here was the real loss. Each astronaut spoke about how they had been inspired toward space exploration or science at a young age; how the gift of a telescope, an interest in animals or a fascination with Apollo missions started them on their journey. These people were, by any measure, highly successful products of an educational system — albeit one from India, another Israel. They had traveled to outer space as a result of individual achievement, and like Icarus, smitten by the power of flight, circled just a little too close to the sun.

But they did, at least, achieve their dream, play mightily on the way. Humankind has always wanted to fly since first spying a bird, just as these astronauts claim their mind was broken open by a youthful fascination.

These things are universal, not preventable. But what gets him — or her — to their destination? To judge by their comments, or to read the Wright Brothers or other pioneers of last century, it was "imagination," a natural curiosity — the singular drive to see if it was possible to fly, go into space or walk the moon. They saw possibilities and potential where others did not. Underlying this imaginative persistence, like so many personal endeavors, is a wondrous and thrilling conviction: seeing what the mind imagines brought to life is the most enjoyable way to spend time on this planet (even if it means flying to another one). Artists are busying themselves the world over on this right now. Many teachers work beyond reason on the challenge of growing ideas and abilities in others. Young students are smitten by chosen subjects in unusual ways every day. A person comes to see that the desired end they are pursuing — writing a poem, excelling at sport, finding a cure for polio — is play in its most enticing form, precisely because they want to know if they can make it happen. And in this sense, for that lucky multitude who inveigle a match between a vocation and what they most love to do, work becomes child's play.

* * *

What youngsters play at an early age — and that they play — can have a profound impact on their life. What starts as innocent fun develops further dimensions and becomes something wholly unexpected. Basketball has been that kind of a thing for me: a vast source of play and also a great teacher. From a very young age, I used to dribble for hours and shoot baskets behind the garage or at the playground and was an early tornado on elementary teams. A sixth grade team photo from 1972 at Swanson-Highland Elementary in South Bend is a classic of Hoosier basketball: two rows of thin white kids, a couple wearing geeky-looking glasses, the lot of us as uncomfortable in saggy uniforms as new army recruits. We were a decent team, won more than we lost, and it wouldn't be bragging to claim I was part of it. All of my play as a tot added up to a precocious kid who knew what to do on a court.

For some reason, I have clear recollections about one game we played against a predominately black elementary school to our north. They had an old gym with high windows and ample rows of bleachers. The benches were directly below their fans; to my surprise the crowd was substantial — many students, parents and apparently, cousins. This was my first experience with black people, and though I didn't feel any sense of revulsion or concern — we had a game to play — my eyes were opened soon enough. Things got beyond us in a hurry. Every time I turned, one of their players was swooping to the basket for a goal. They pressed us and we couldn't seem to get the ball across half-court without it squirting loose, the lot of us turning tail to play defense. One kid, Maurice Hardiman, at least six feet tall with condor arms, jumped right over us when we inconvenienced him by being in his way. He had a generous afro, black-rimmed glasses like Malcolm X, square shoulders and a demeanor a lot tougher than any of us. Several times he drove to the hoop or followed up shots at the rim as the crowd exploded. We lost by 40 points. I wasn't so much disappointed as awestruck; this team dwarfed us, making us seem like boyscouts of basketball make-believe.

That next year at Clay Junior High, crossroads for a number of South Bend's elementaries, there were two basketball teams, but for some reason, even though there were blacks at school, including Maurice Hardiman, each squad remained exclusively white. In fact, I can scarcely remember seeing, talking to or having blacks in any of my classes. My time at Clay took on a familiar pattern. I spent morning and afternoon trying to find something riveting to focus on without much success. In between, instead of eating lunch, I went to an adjacent gym for an hour of basketball, an all-against-everyone donnybrook called *Wild 21*. Basically, this meant dropping a ball amongst caged animals and letting them determine the course of evolution by who could get it through the cylinder most.

One day something happened. A friend asked me if I knew where Maurice was, that people were looking for him. We weren't fast friends but had a kind of understanding from playing basketball together that served as our bond. I remember passing by the double-doors and looking down a long hallway, seeing Maurice there on the floor, with three grown men led by Mr. Thornton — the arch vice-principal — holding him as he struggled. A lump went up and down my throat. What were they doing to him? And why? The bell rang and I moved on to another part of the building so I never got good answers; I am not even sure I ever saw Maurice again or if he returned to school. At this point he fades from my memory. But I had a visceral feeling of ugliness thrust into the equation that day, a force precisely the opposite of play. To me, it related to Maurice being black, while the rest of us — including those in charge — were white.

* * *

In 1976, I went almost three months without talking to anyone at Burlington High School in Vermont. I was the new kid, and despite endless nattering of freshman girls around my locker, I was determined to remain silent. Then junior-varsity basketball began and my whole dismal destiny dissolved in front of me. A raft of new people came into view — teammates, coaches, cheerleaders, parents. The possibility that life might lead somewhere emerged from behind clouds as our first "B-squad" game drew near. I went home that day after school, lay down in the living room with a ball, shot it up in the air over and over as I listened to Led Zeppelin, visualizing this game's importance. I think I even prayed.

We were in Winooski that night playing the Spartans. Their backcourt was composed of identical twins, which made it hard because you had to look at their numbers. I just watched the ball, mentally whispering "Gimme that," making steal after steal, missing as many lay-ups as I made, getting fouled, clanking the rim with free-throws but coaxing more than a few to go in. In many ways, except for the chagrin I felt missing so many shots, it was a dream game. We won fairly comfortably and when the mist of post-game showers cleared, Coach Hanbridge sat me down to reveal a discrepancy about what I had done: our book had me for 30 points. The official one, Winooski's, had me at 35. I sighed. This was going to be better than I anticipated.

That spring I got called up to sit on the varsity bench while they made a playoff run. It was a senior-dominated team; they were highly ranked and it was retirement year for their dinosaur of a coach, Mr. Burke. He was a wonderful gentleman and instructor, with more than 25 years in the business, and had been there my first day at Burlington to welcome me, introduce himself, invite me to try out. Portly with a military haircut, he kept a white towel on his lap during games, which he chewed on if things got tense. One after another we rattled off wins against lower division teams — newspapers playing up the angle of Coach Burke's final year — until we found ourselves standing alone against Springfield for the 1977 Vermont State Championship.

This was a great vicarious experience for me, but the doe-eyed, even-keeled seniors felt a stultifying pressure as game-time approached down in the locker room. Our 6'7" center, who had a scholarship to Maine, looked pale as a warm lobster and sat for a time in the bathroom stall. The senior guards dribbled nervously in the hallway, trying to get the right feel. Things were quiet, tense, Burke chewing away before game-time. But there was one kid, Mike Hartnett, who walked in with a broad smile on his face. He was the wild card on this squad; only 6'1" as a forward, left-handed, given to flights of fancy which could drive a coach crazy. (Burke got in his face more than once for being too casual.) He had longish hair that swept off to the side, a devilish smile and deep dimples beneath blue eyes. Generally, he was the garbage man, the player who mops up, catches a long outlet pass or hammers home a jump shot with no one on him.

There was this uncanny confidence about him that day, this joy that he was about to play the biggest game of his life. He was the only player willing to talk before tip-off. I felt encouraged about this but also a little wary — he wasn't what you would call real bright. Amazing though, he stepped on the floor, the first play of the game swung his way, and he put up a long jump-shot. Bang! He hit his first three and many more, scoring 23 points, a pillar of stability as other Burlington players fouled out, got wobbly and gave ground. It was a great match, up and down, back and forth. From the front row, I saw how this kid won a state championship for us because he had a mental framework so entirely beyond — or underneath — everyone else and which basically said: "This is all about play, the one damn thing I can do in life."

That was the summit for me with basketball. The last two years of high school were filled more with anxiety, pressure and responsibility than the unfettered release of play. In fact, because of other concerns — academics, relationships, counter-culture — at a certain point, I didn't have much interest. Neither did I possess joints or muscles which allowed for a daily pounding. I didn't especially care for teammates, despised the unyielding schedule, rolled my eyes at the folderol of school spirit, cheerleaders, press coverage. "Who cares?" was my prevalent attitude. It wasn't any fun.

* * *

I understand now that playing, whether sports or cards or building snowmen, is more about metaphor than outcome; more about encounter and its lessons than success or failure, the winning and losing so closely followed by partisans on either side. I understand, but it still hurts for me to lose at anything, even just a match of backgammon over beers with my very lovely wife. Competition is intense, a spontaneous process which, as the Greeks believed, should bring out our best, not just in physical excellence but in heart and mind as well. That didn't happen for me in high school and it has left a kind of scar: questions about my identity and the sharpness of my competitive edge.

Each of us must come to peace with the terms of our involvement in competition. There are deep reasons to play, and despite Vince Lombardi's telling quote, "Winning isn't everything; it's the only thing", millions — even billions — continue to believe in the purity of this pursuit by turning up at a field, laughing or dancing through warm-ups, trying out a new handshake on their opponent and not possessing any larger purpose than seeing what kind of inventiveness they can lure from their body. This is their best get-away from the self who sits and wonders and languishes, constrained by limitations of work or family or obligation. For a time at least, there are no messy diapers, financial pressures, nor rotting wood at the homestead; no real need to do other than chase back and forth — lunging, laughing, cringing and howling.

I may be wrong about this, off by a couple billion or so, but I swear by the implications behind it. Play is essentially about hope, love for the care-free feel of youth, the possibility that something magic might visit at any moment, mirroring the experience of a wild, beating heart. It is an infinitely optimistic enterprise which posits that there is time enough for a satisfying diversion from the main road. Or perhaps, that the main road *is about diversion* after all — the one sure way we can engage with life, gauge its strength and passion. We don't question it when young, picking it up naturally, without pretense. And we certainly don't give much thought, before it actually happens, to growing old and being unable to play physically anymore. But then, things don't always turn out as we plan. The body grows old even while the heart stays young. That's why, more often than not, we chuck it and determine just to play; play for as long as we can.

I never gave up on basketball, despite the sour resolution I came to in high school. Wherever I found myself summers, I courted playgrounds to mix it up with whites and blacks playing street ball. At college, I was on intramural teams and coached at an elementary school. Over the last decades, every winter has found me in church basements or gymnasiums late at night fully engaged, looking for my rhythm. It's a part of me that is familiar, has the memory of my physical body in it, and along with writing and family, I need to remind me who I am.

At De La Salle I coached freshman basketball for four years. It was a small assignment, though having won the State Championship the year before I started and being a kind of basketball magnet lent as much gravitas as I would have wanted. In typical fashion, De La Salle asked the coach to do more than humanly possible: assigning players a study hall *in your room* after school, requiring that *you* drive a small bus to and from practice, that *you* set up the gym on game days, tape ankles, sweep the gym-floor, find someone to keep the official book.

I enjoyed coaching, but I also came away with a feeling that something is clearly wrong in our mixing of sport and school. We give generous scholarships to athletes who are less than generous human beings, passing over deserving candidates who have worked hard and contribute greatly to their communities. It is well-documented that big-time college sports (mainly men's basketball and football) are not only destructive to individuals it chews up and spits out, but also to institutions imprudent enough to chase athletic success and increased alumni donations. Dollars are invested to breed more dollars while humans fall as detritus off to the side. It is indeed a fool's wager, millions spent, whole facilities and programs created, not in an effort to sponsor a greater sense of play but in vain hopes of making money. The pressure to win, to become a "perennial power-house," reverberates backward into high school where youngsters take up the call as the next prized recruit, sacrificing academics to this single-minded pursuit; parents all too willing to sacrifice blood and treasure for the glory of their good name. This is the real wasteful fun in schools around the country. When will we hear calls for "accountability" and "standards" in the athletic programs of our schools and universities?

How extraordinarily far we have come from the days of a peach basket on the gym wall and a bunch of kids screwing around most of an afternoon. How remarkably far we have come in my lifetime, when baby-boom children needed only a frozen pond or a wobbly backboard; and professional sports — while important and entertaining — were not multi-billion dollar industries whose influence pushed their way deep into the economic vitals of our economy.

How far we have come from that December night in 1989 when I pulled the bus up at Brooklyn Center High School and led an unpredictable squad of freshman into the very building where, the year before, I had been a student teacher. This team had some kind of magic and chemistry. Our starting five was a black kid from the projects, a gangly Hispanic from Guatemala, an African named Kao, a chunky Italian forward whose parents owned a restaurant, and a white center whose dad was a judge. Off the bench, we brought a Mexican left-handed shooter named Che, an adopted Korean big man, a hip-hop mixed-raced kid quick as blazes, plus a wide assortment of grammar-school survivors. I marched them into the locker room, Brooklyn Center students giving us wide berth. Our season was still a developing thing, we had won one game and lost one.

Our special defense was a trapping zone that started the other side of half-court with our quickest athletes. We smothered them — as the black team had us in Indiana — a heavy blanket tossed over the team huddle. I am not even sure what the score was, not close, but I was talking to one of my players in the 4th quarter about a bad shot when the referee gave me a technical foul: the only one I ever got as a coach. "For what?" I asked. He proceeded to lecture me in a loud, angry voice, which everyone could hear, about running up the score, how unethical I was to be pouring it on like this. I looked at my bench; all my reserves were in the game. "What are you talking about?" I was livid. My face flushed; my throat tightened. My whole team was watching. He was obviously a booster or a parent, and he took his one chance to strike back at us, at me, for the thorough drubbing his boys were getting.

I see now that it was not the time or place to advocate for justice — no one felt bad for us just then — though he went far beyond his role as official in berating me. This could have been a thinly veiled outburst of racism. I had done nothing wrong; neither had my team. At the time I sat down and shut up, though in many ways, I felt like I was backing down when I most needed to stand up for myself and my players. We weren't in the world so Mr. Official could use us a washrag for his own frustration. My face burned red. Almost every bit of good feeling about the game and my life drained out of me just then, like I was tangling with something old and unmanageable. I felt as if I were failing, once again, to rise to a public moment with the conviction and poise required of my position. I walked to the locker-room beaten, as if we were the ones who had just been humiliated.

Afterwards, we ran out to the bus. It was below zero and windy. I cranked it over and over but it wouldn't go. Flooded. This happened; it was an old bus. I waited and tried again. Still nothing. I noticed too, much to my consternation, that the cranking power was lessening — not as much oomph as the first time I turned it. A few more tries and my fears were realized: the battery died. "Mr. Henry, it's cold!" The cheerleaders still had skirts on. I got down, looked around. It was just into twilight, an empty tundra stretched on all sides, our bus a small yellow dinosaur in the vast parking lot. Kao was walking to his parent's car. I yelled to him, asking for a jump-start. They pull up in this rusty Dodge Dart, a thing of beauty just then, especially with its jumper cables and crummy little battery.

We pop the bus hood, a couple of curious kids stand up on the bumper to watch. But then, a surprise: no battery. "What?" I think out loud, batting arms against myself. "There has to be a battery." We initiate a search and after a bit, the Delmonicos call out from the driver's side. "We found it! We found it!" Sure enough, a little panel lifts up and a tray in there slides out with a battery on it. We hook it up to the Dart, and Kao's dad, an African who barely speaks English, revs the engine.

After a few minutes, I turn the key. Nothing, not even a hack. I get off the bus, take down the cables. "We're done," I think. We'll have to call school or take a city bus or maybe even taxis. I suddenly have 20 very good reasons to worry about what we do next. I review the money in my wallet — nothing but a few dollar bills. But then, I have a brain-storm, something that proves, perhaps clear as anything, that your background growing up — that "inner landscape" — is what makes or breaks you working with kids. Teachers are made long before they ever set foot in a classroom. The rightness of a particular moment and uniqueness in your character make a match; it's not something you can simulate or train for. "Everyone off the bus," I command. The cheerleaders don't budge. I explain that I mean *everyone*, that we are going to push and can't afford to have any extra weight on board. This came out badly — "No one is saying you're over-weight" — several of them seem hurt as they step to the parking lot. The younger Delmonico kid looks at me in a sad way as if undoing my delusion: "Mr. Henry, it's too far to push." De La Salle is out there 6 to 8 miles. I explain that we're just going to try this last ditch maneuver, that everyone needs to go back and dig in.

This was a pinnacle of achievement for me as a young instructor, barely an hour after I was sure that I had been humiliated for all time. Twenty kids, mostly inner-city and bundled awkwardly against the cold, pushed a dilapidated bus around an empty suburban lot seemingly stuck with misfortune, their improvisational coach dithering away, grasping at straws. As they got up to a steady crawl, I dropped it into second, let the clutch out and turned the key — the engine fired clean. A muffled roar dimly penetrated from outside. I flipped open the door and smiled as they filed on faster than ever. I tried hard to look non-chalant gearing it out to the road, turning toward home, kids settling in for the ride — but inside, I was pumping fists like I had just made good on every jump-shot since puberty.

* * *

I will always love to play: to race through woods on skis, to fling horse-shoes at steel stakes, to unfold my hand in a game of Hearts. I enjoy movies and music and meal time at a nice restaurant. I am fond of street action around a stadium, the relaxed play in parks, the flicks of eye-contact riding a subway. And I especially love the play that I feel in young people — their happy toss into the fray of being alive, willing to create fun almost anywhere. Children, more than anyone, know how to have fun, and I honestly believe that this precise quality, having never been completely broken from my identity, is what allows me to enjoy being around them now, to smile and believe we are just about to embark on something especially playful. I learned it young and have continued to chase it as the central point of being alive.

If I haven't convinced the reader by now that play is the heart and soul of education and a good life, not to mention a growing obsession in America, I likely never will. But two more things. When leaders in our country were looking to integrate blacks into mainstream America, where did they turn? Jackie Robinson and baseball. It was not smooth, easy or without pain; but rather, visible, public and all-important. And it sure worked. Jackie demonstrated that he, and many blacks, could play America's game — all of America's games. The integration of Little Rock High School, University of Alabama and dozens of lunch counters across the south did not go as well, with National Guardsmen rolling up in troop transports and police chiefs addressing white mobs over bullhorns. Meanwhile, black activists and marchers were regularly tear-gassed, fire-hosed and beaten. None of this was fun, nor equal, nor fair. There is some-thing special about play, something riveting, fanciful, and despite the authority of umpires and referees, even harmonious. I never really grasped the overall significance of play in my life or in our society until trying to tackle it in this chapter. Now everywhere I look, I see evidence of its long, dominating shadow.

When I first started teaching at Park Center in the then mostly white suburb of Brooklyn Park — it, like most of America has changed quickly in the last decade in terms of race — there was a sizeable portion of black kids, especially young men, hanging out between class near the cafeteria. They seemed completely out of place, talking loud and slapping hands, smiling big, getting their raps on. I knew from a counselor in the office that there was not one of these dozens of kids in the top 50 percent of our school's graduating class. Not one. Black-on-black crime seemed to be getting worse. Gangs were a genuine threat. Images of black men as perpetrators of violence, drugs and crime filled the media. This disturbed me, as it did portions of the community and some on the teaching staff. I didn't know many of these youngsters well, but in another way, I felt like I knew them all. I imagined that I saw Maurice there, and Greg, my black backcourt partner from high school; Marcel, a Camerounian friend I met in France, and Ernest, a young man I knew from playing ball at a Minneapolis park. I believed these were good kids with a variety of talents and that something valuable was being wasted.

I sometimes imagine that African-American have a greater penchant for play than others. I sense that in their love of language, music, sports and dance; in their rich heritage of spirituality, art and overcoming hardship inflicted by centuries of slavery and official racism. It is not something I need to prove: stereotyping any group or individual is inherently dangerous and likely to fail. I should know because it was entirely improbable that a white child born in the racially isolated enclave of St. Cloud would work for racial understanding, steer classes directly into issues of diversity and fight a school bureaucracy to create an African-American literature class. But that is exactly where I ended up: in a suburb engulfed by rapid change, desperately in need of new programs and approaches. What business of this was mine? I had minimal experience with race issues, scant knowledge of America's uneven history toward blacks, little familiarity with stories, plays or poetry celebrating what Langston Hughes called "the darker brother." It wasn't any of my business; at least, that's the message I got from the principal who recommended against the creation of an African-American literature class — though it eventually won approval higher up. It became my business because I wanted it to, because I sensed unfairness, a racial awkwardness as surely in the 1990s as during my youth. I accessed this conviction originally through play, a venue where, unlike so many, Americans generally have equal opportunity.

My best efforts, including the literature course I created, have not meant an end to underachievement amongst that group of young men around the cafeteria, nor significantly altered a problematic racial divide within the community of Brooklyn Park. Neither has all the cooperative group-work in my few English classes undone the racial suspicion and distrust amongst kids, as if school alone can change the cultural landscape. Numbers of blacks and immigrants have continued to grow in our district and so have needs for additional programming and approaches. The virtues and success of my efforts have been small scale, helping students — white and black — one at a time, and mostly girls, the more dependable gender when it comes to appreciating literature. That's one thing about employing play as a jumping off point for a larger agenda: you can never be too sure about the final result.

no sex, no drugs, no rock 'n roll

I learned a startling truth at school in third or fourth grade. Madison Elementary was across from our bulging bulwark in St. Cloud where nine children waddled down the plank every morning like Ping in the child's tale about a Chinese duck boat, returning faithfully each night before my father pulled up boards and secured the latch. There is a concrete ramp at Madison running west to east, not unlike the plank of that story, leading up to glass doors and a hallway that stretches for almost a block into the rest of the building. Cool kids, rebels and those with nothing better to do made a habit of sitting under "the ramp"; it sheltered us from weather, provided cover for activities that might get us branded as deviants. It was here, surrounded by older boys that I first held a smoke and learned, to my shock, that adults, including my own upright, Catholic and very non-sexual parents, made a habit of intercourse. At first, I denied this. The unbearable weight of something so dirty and debased as sex between my parents suffocated me. But slowly it dawned that in fact this must be true, that I had been living all this time in enchanted ignorance: surrounded by siblings with odd parts of Mom and Dad that represented nothing less than a spree of sexual profligacy.

A year or two later, Billy McKinney and a buddy showed up at our door, their bikes ditched next to my brother's inoperable Karmann Ghia in the driveway. They had something to talk about. Yesterday, Billy said with self-importance, he had been with 7th graders behind the junior high where Cindy Plepsen and Mary Schmidt allowed him to pinch their boobs. Short, dishwater blond, with stringy hair, something about not having a father or reliable teeth made Billy seem tough. His story had a tail, too. Apparently, later that night, with the help of beer, Billy had been with other girls, out-of-towners. When he got to this part, his friend took over, an out-of-the-neighborhood guy himself; impartiality was needed. "We were over at Miller's house, in the trailer, and ah, there were some girls there. And Billy finger-banged this girl." Finger-bang, he said; I remember that. I nodded, not having any idea what I had just acceded to. Wow, quite a weekend, Billy. I did the only thing I knew how to at that point: went in to finish the baseball game I was watching.

A couple of months after that, supine in the porch of our lake home, I discovered that rubbing myself wrapped up in a sleeping bag got to feeling better the more I did it. Things got out of hand at some point and my body, for the first time since sneezes and vomit, propagated its own agenda. Like Billy's stories, I had no idea about right or wrong, only a clumsy impression that something alluring and tingly came into my body. It wasn't unnatural, but then, neither did I have full possession of it. Now, decades later, a clearer picture has emerged: We grow up bathing in an amniotic pool of darkness, only to be ejected in spurts and involuntary spasms, left to swim our way out of childhood into a distinctly adult universe — governed by Eros — itself originally conceived as part of some "big-bang." We don't talk much about the journey; it's mysterious, most often discovered alone — a private burden of give and take, control and submission, smooth skin and bumpy rides. And no school will get you there in total purity or unblemished virtue, except the one delivering hard knocks.

* * *

I suppose anyone who spends their first 20 years growing up in the '60s and '70s can be forgiven for forming the wrong impression of what life is about. Listening to America's music scene alone was grounds for seduction, if not outright deception. Jimi Hendrix, Janis Joplin, Joni Mitchell, The Doors, Bob Dylan, Joan Baez, Buffalo Springfield, Jefferson Airplane, (to name a few) made it seem like you died and went to heaven before being old enough to drink. Iconoclastic, combating the status quo, seeking transformation of mind and society, most of it asks and promises "revolution," leaving the accumulated impression that America was on the verge of immense change. Paradoxically, at times that change intertwines with narcissistic impulses to consume — to imbibe of America's utopic freedom, at others, to sacrifice every last shred for important social causes. No wonder the '60s legacy creates such sharp battle lines: Vietnam, flower power, Woodstock, women's liberation, communes, pot-smoking, the Stonewall Inn, Earthday, long hair, Black Panthers, dropping out, turning on, VW vans, demonstrations where vocalists shouted "Fuck Nixon" and "Drop Acid" in the same breath — these are historic shards which endure and provoke polemics. And whichever way you think they may have tried to pull the table cloth — toward themselves or on behalf of others — I want to acknowledge that generation's singular achievement: they made great music.

Some want to believe that the "liberation" and individual excesses, including music, of two consecutive decades have everything to do with what is bad in contemporary America: a naïve liberalism tending to "blame

America first" while overcompensating with social programs indenturing the poor to government handouts, leading downhill to race-based admissions, sexual hedonism, rampant drugs, and disastrous schools ruled by permissiveness. (Strong stuff from people who, in the next breath, hail us as "The greatest nation on earth.") These faults stem from the "original sin" of the '60s, bucking the track that previous generations had created with hard work, sacrifice and delay of gratification. Luckily, in this view, Ronald Reagan restored order, started us on regaining honor and purpose. In his divine authority, he stomped out drugs and reduced teenage pregnancy by uttering, along with his wife, a single, childlike word: "No." No sex, no drugs, no rock n' roll. It's that easy.

I can't say I am a big fan of Ronald Reagan, but anyone in my class has heard this many, many times, "No sex, no drugs, no rock n' roll," because it's my final admonition before sending them from the room with an open-ended journal topic. After awhile, a cheerful handful even join me as if it has become one of their favorite refrains: "*No sex, drugs or rock n'roll!*" I have determined, though, that this works only partially. Either social critics have it right or Reagan got it wrong because a majority of young people, whether they admit it or not, want to talk drugs, sex and rock n' roll, especially when you tell them not to.

As a matter of fact, most writers hoping to sell a good number of books are required to follow a certain formula: one that Ron and Nancy, if they were with us, might acknowledge reveals a disturbing contradiction about our society. Whatever the story, even if it is about a good-natured parish priest (or especially these days), you will need to include some racy sex scenes. Also, incorporate plenty of violence, then reference the lusty fury and overall athletic-ness of those racy sex scenes. Mix in drug or alcohol abuse, or just shabby behavior involving more sex or suggestions of it — this time sandwiched around disturbing cruelty, vivid and raw. Midway or sooner, throw in a murder, preferably just after a previously unknown sex act is discovered, then set about solving it in the least way likely. This can be done with sophistication and finesse à la Cheever or Updike, or roughly, matter-of-fact in the grind it out world of petty criminals à la Elmore Leonard. Mass market? Leave that to romance writers.

Either way, publishers know what sells books. And magazines. And movies. And music. And especially television programs. We're back to one word here, Ron and Nancy, the one you don't want to hear at a time like this: a pushy boyfriend, drug pusher, or the person next to you breathing heavily. "Sex" Say it in a hushed, breathy way: "S-E-X". Sex, drugs and rock n' roll. "YES." It gets said every day, probably with increasing frequency, no matter who occupies the White House or what we teach children. This is the great undertow of America's culture, framed in glossy magazines, lit up in neon, beamed to the silver screen and throbbing from every over-powered sub-woofer on the parkway. This stuff is not only in our genes — and in our jeans — it's become the marketing engine of an entire commercial culture for one extremely good reason: It works! I need to admit right now that I have been compelled to write this chapter under pressure that this topic, and this topic alone, will make my manuscript commercially viable. I confess in advance that this chapter is not a consensual act.

* * *

Bodies. What an inconvenience, especially at my age. The aches, odd cracking of joints and loss of so many faculties I once took for granted. For teenagers, the ones taking them for granted, what a marvelous apparatus. All parts in working order, some in top form, others barely used. Most young adults look great, even though they don't deserve it for all the shit-food they consume. There can be no denying that of the many things teenagers do not possess with any skill or worth, bodies are not among them. Witness high school sports: so talented, so much cockiness and such evident joy. Boys and girls jump and hit and run better than ever. A fortunate few are even provided further opportunity to do it at college on a scholarship. Or witness high school musicals or orchestra or dance lines. More bodies with talent and discipline. More scholarships. Or, if you prefer, just stand around a typical American high school and watch. All shapes, all sizes; length and strength, grace and race; more head then a haunch, bigger butt than a paunch; legs and arms and ears; noses and hips and mouths. All kinds; everywhere. More clothing and less than ever, pants to the knees, shirts above the belly button, bra straps and briefs with labels out like what we are really doing here is modeling lingerie and underwear.

The basic conflict is that we live in a youth-oriented culture. Marketers of products understand, take advantage of and cater to it. There is a gold mine out there in terms of sales. Young people represent not just a high consuming demographic, but because of brand loyalty and their long tenure as future consumers, *the most important market* in America. Teens dress in ways created exclusively by main stream apparel and media conglomerates. Soft drinks, music, sneakers are all packaged as the coolest of cool. Youngsters appear composed about it all. And in fact, they have all the parts of a certifiable adult. Unfortunately, they have roughly half the common sense and know-how — and none of the rights, privileges or responsibility — a sure prescription for shabby behavior. It's like putting a kid behind the wheel of a fancy car: CD player, tachometer, 400 horses, the smell of leather, a hard-blowing heater, good rubber, and a springy gas pedal which makes it all really go. Now tell them they shouldn't drive or even want to drive, that they don't know how. Tell them they are wrong, bad, dirty to want to drive that silly car. Tell them that they are not free to do what they want and under no circumstances should they insert the key — at least not until married or they own it themselves. We know what happens. Tires squeal through the night.

Here's a durable dogma koan: Want to get kids interested? Tell them something is off-limits. That they shouldn't consider it. Not to think about it, wonder about it, look at it, touch it, run their fingers along it, hold it, squeeze it, love it, or secretly get obsessed by it. The bare fact is: Telling kids "no," and especially "no way" or "no how" without significant explanation or a real relationship functions as one giant invitation to give it a try. By the way, don't read any further. Ever. You aren't mature enough.

* * *

I learned to drive myself, at an appropriate age, though this was no luxury affair — just a '72 Dodge Valiant. I know it looks primitive by today's standards, but I loved that car. (Full disclosure: it was owned by my parents.) I read once that 1972 was the exact apex of America's power, and that since then, economically and culturally, it's been downhill. Well, this was tops for sure: fatigue green, slant six, four doors, plenty of room on cloth seats, shaped like a moving bread box and every bit as dependable. It was my daily bread. And also, on weekends, my nightly bed (or knightly bed) for late-night trysts with my girlfriend Sarah. A six-pack of Miller was all the fuel we needed. Little soldiers fell one-by-one into the back as we conducted maneuvers, parked in an obscure neighborhood, windows fogged — bodies, skin, lips anxious for touch.

Sarah was a year older and wiser. She lived at the end of Cross Street, in a cul-de-sac, her mom a kind of conservative Christian way before her time. That troubled me and also, in my hyper-symbolic state of mind, that their road was marked "Dead End." I can't explain why that mattered: some fatalistic belief that small things add up and always point to something crucial. In fact, several months into our romance, I took the liberty of removing that sign, gathering together the requisite tools and a step-ladder and posing as a city worker doing maintenance — at 1 o'clock in the morning. After some minor setbacks, I managed to get it down, resounding in an alien "twang." I smuggled it home in my Valiant (oh, the symbolic value of my car's name!), where it took up residence on the wall above my bed, proof that some things are more about will than fate.

Sarah was a cheerleader; I played basketball. At first we were friends, teasing constantly, driving Burlington as we sifted through family issues and hopes for college, neither of us real good at "fitting in." That connected us. To most kids in Vermont, I was still the transplant from Missouri, er, Montana, er someplace out west. Sarah's father had died of a heart attack when she was eight, leaving her brother and a reclusive mother to muddle through on Social Security. We talked openly, felt good about knocking down walls, those social, emotional constructs which have us passing by without seeming to care. Her neck-length brown hair curled in on itself and her large brown eyes, which she crossed regularly in the cutest way. She was no glamour girl, but had a taut, muscular frame and the daring-do for splits and jumps and formations during time-outs.

I was doltish, lacked confidence and couldn't identify a sexual indicator unless it was graphic and in a magazine or done with bold lettering, at least the size of that Dead End sign. And that's what it took sometime in January after one of our games. Our team was in the midst of a long winning streak, highly ranked — the kind of hubris that tends to blind. There was a keg party at Wallace's, our red-headed klutz of a center. We resorted to the usual devices, drinking and smoking as a snow squall swept through Burlington dropping a powder load. Revelry went past midnight, right through Sarah's concerted attempts to wish me goodnight. When I reached my Valiant, there were symbols shrouded in snow but unmistakable on my windshield: just three of them — two vowels, I and U, and a heart in-between. "What the hell?" I thought; I never felt so dumb in my life. Snow blew off the bread box as I spun around onto the boulevard, speeding to North Avenue then Cross Street, dazzling intersections lit by heavy flakes. It seemed like I was speeding into a mysterious yet well-known dream, that feeling again: a tingly nervousness way bigger than me. Racing to the end, I found Sarah waltzing on the walk like she had been waiting hours for a decent pair of lights. I left my engine running, never closed my door as she came to me without words. Snow whitened our hair in minutes, melted on steamed faces and ran icily down to cool jumpy fires within. The Dead End had a hell of a beginning.

* * *

Rather than us both avoiding the topic and being so secretly fascinated that we are devastated by it as a marketing tool, maybe everyone should be encouraged to recall early sexual experiences and share them. That would be a start to tackling fear, denial and allure for an issue which, one way or another, makes a lot of cheeks red. Mine, like most, would not be so glorious or romantic as with Sarah — nor as crass and unfeeling as what I heard from Billy. In South Bend, playing post-office in 7th grade at Lori Renard's house under the watchful eyes of her parents. Lori says behind the curtain: "I want you to know that I only called you in here so that you could call Nikki in next; she likes you." Nikki is a friend, a nice catch but nothing compared to Lori, who dates high-schoolers. I nod dumbly as she drills me with her juicy lips, pushing young breasts forward and temporarily using my forwarding address on Nikki's behalf. In Burlington, the first penetration (not Sarah) ends in tears and upset (and nothing more) as a sophomore at a cabin in the woods; in an interesting reversal, the bloody sheet is hauled to a washing machine to conceal, not reveal, the reality of lost virginity. I even got tossed out of Sarah's house one time when her mom, the Christian, came home and found us looking awkward and disheveled in the basement. What would Jesus have done, Mrs. C?

There are only 5 essential needs in human beings: air, water, sleep, food and sex. I list them in descending order of importance for survival, but reverse order of daily interest and attention. A person has only minutes without air, days without water or sleep, several weeks (if they are healthy) without food, but somehow, in the estimation of many parents, can go for 27 years — which is now the average age of first marriage — without sex. Catholic priests notwithstanding, there are some ascetics, mystics and others, disturbed or disciplined, who probably can survive that long without sex. Gandhi himself forswore it, believing that "vital fluids" strengthened body and spirit and maybe they do. (Of course, he also slept with women naked to continually refine his powers.)

If you live in or visit an American metropolis, take a look in the back of one of those arts and entertainment weeklies piled free at the entrances to restaurants, theaters and shopping centers. Turn to the back, peruse the want ads (and I do mean "want" ads): the phone sex solicitations, escort services, singles ads. Here is America's sexual market-place, page after page of dense material. We have a kind of sexual revolution seeping its way under the door of America's suburban utopia. (And apparently, some pretty major addictions.) Most people sense this already if they watch T.V., surf the Web, walk shopping malls or visit Las Vegas — where yellow pages list hundreds and hundreds of professional "entertainers." Or, even if they just analyze the motel/hotel association's revenue figures, where adult pay-per-view programming — read, 'porn' — is the fastest growing segment in the industry.

There are some parents, politicians and ministers who seem genuinely upset about this. In the late 1990s, there was a parent-based movement to reform the sex-education curriculum in my district. A small, dedicated group of conservatives fought their way onto a committee, ramming through a program which provides a choice for students — and especially parents. Sophomores can now take an abstinence-based curriculum, which strongly recommends abstinence but provides full information about sexual and reproductive issues, including diseases, contraception and homosexuality. Or they can sign up for Abstinence Until Marriage, which does not give information about reproduction other than the magic formula the Reagans used to immortalize their agenda: "*Just Say No.*" No information about homosexuality, none about transmitted diseases, nothing on contraception, not even a hint as to where babies come from. None of these issues even exist as long as you are safely in the room and the teacher follows the script (and not all of them do).

I respect the rights of parents to inform their child about sex. That has always been an option in our district, to pull a son or daughter during parts of the course you find objectionable or contrary to religious conviction. That's not what this is. This new course is about truly believing that young people stand a better chance of success in the 21st century *if they are ignorant rather than informed.* The arrogance of this is remarkable. Why the state of Minnesota does not see a compelling interest in making sure citizens, particularly those entering their sexually active, child-rearing years, have basic information about reproductive issues is bewildering beyond my powers of explanation. The underlying premise seems to be that what went wrong with the '60's and '70s was that young people were given too free a reign, too much access to risky attitudes and ideas. Remove the temptation that such diabolical material provides and you have a solution for America's sexual appetites — at least amongst teens.

And that this kind of brainwashing is done under the rubric of providing students "a choice" is a chimera. Someone is always in charge of innocent minds: God Himself, Satan, or in this case, parents. I have conducted planning sessions going over the health/sex-ed option. Parents want to believe there is a magic bullet out there, a potion that will drowse their child over the hump between adolescence and safe marriage. In their mind, they don't want *any* sexual issues involving their youngster. They were just a baby after all, so cute, so innocent, and before that, well... again, time to face facts, Mr. and Mrs. America — an unexplainable instance of your own sexual impulse. In a matter of seconds they scribble in *Abstinence Until Marriage* on the course registration without so much as a discussion. The student hunches her shoulders grittily, trying not to roll eyes in front of me — like any indication of dissent is proof of sexual deviousness. I smile. Cheer up, kid. It's an easy class.

This type of abstinence orthodoxy, along with efforts by local churches to institute mass-abstinence pledges among youth is open for debate as to effectiveness, at least in the mainstream media. I've read articles claiming that disease and pregnancy rates shoot up with the onset of such programs; I've also heard conservatives claim they have incontrovertible proof that abstinence works. (Good for them! Abstinence works all right; until it fails, then all hell breaks loose.) If an individual or couple want to forego sexual activity, that's certainly an option, but why confuse it with public policy or effective education? In my classroom over the last five years, and this is admittedly anecdotal — teenage pregnancy rates are down on a national level — pregnancies, which had never been an issue during my first 10 years of teaching, skyrocketed from none to a dozen. Many factors could explain this, but it is nonetheless heart-wrenching, a clear sign of something dreadfully wrong: children, not yet educated or personally competent, having more children.

We need to acknowledge a fundamental truth about education: schools do not alter wider trends and developments in society (and neither can music) as much as we suppose — a wistful fantasy because we spend such large sums on them. They are much more *reflective* of social trends. And how completely ironic that some critics decry the essential ineffectiveness of government programs — especially schools when it comes to teaching basics — but turn on a dime to fault public education for efficacy in inculcating loose morals and degenerate behavior through sex ed, as if *it's the one goddamn thing we're good at*! The fact is, sexuality, long suppressed, denied, covered up, is rearing its (perhaps not so ugly?) head in American society and will not simply be nipped in the bud by changes in health curriculum. Although, it is certainly possible that we make things considerably worse by insisting students remain ignorant, without real power or responsibility for their bodies, life or learning.

Not many young people set out to become pregnant or contract a disease; they find their own snaky path to it. I should know. One night in the summer after Sarah graduated from high school, we went on a date. She would be leaving for college in a week; I was now a senior and captain of the basketball team. Like every smooth-jointed, strong-limbed 17 year-old, I was indestructible, invulnerable, undeniably cool. We went to the Chicken Bone for dinner, had a couple of pitchers of beer, maybe even a margarita. (Bookchin's mail-order I.D. worked like a charm.) We headed for the Henry house after, though with my brother gone and parents out of town, we were locked out. No matter. I broke in the back door by tearing out a safety chain — this could be explained later under the right circumstances. We quickly got into bed, my bed, for the first time, tore at each other's clothes, groping and heaving right underneath that Dead End sign. I can't say it was exceptional, but I do know it was worthy of procreation because Sarah called me in December from Boston, where she had just obtained a positive on a pregnancy test.

It felt unearthly big; it still does. We never figured it could happen. Because of an operation as a child, Sarah had been told she could never get pregnant. We were literally fooled by rationalizations, excuses, the "Why this is O.K. right now" — even though it rarely, if ever, is. Being in high school seemed excruciating with my girlfriend in the big city and our would-be child in her belly. I had trouble sleeping, my studies tanked, I couldn't get into playing basketball. High-schoolers put on a good front when they need to, but they have souls and hurt carries a ton more weight when it has never happened before. Sarah and I weren't as close; she'd been gone for three months. We needed to be together, to talk, but time was of the essence (the first trimester thing) and she was far away. My secret was big enough that I couldn't admit it to anyone; not coach, not friends, and certainly not my mom or dad. In their minds, I had no reason to go to Boston just then and I didn't know how to do anything better.

It's not for me to describe the deep power of need, of lust, of love overcoming boundaries and intentions. Just to recognize that I've got it, too. We all do; the human ones anyway. Thus, we wake to find six billion souls tucked in beside us: some conceived in wisdom, some in pain, the majority a result of a profound but unconscious release from routine that overmasters our waking life. Call it biology; call it divine; call it bestial or profane; call it what you will but acknowledge that it is ubiquitous, essential, unstoppable. In the end, Sarah aborted at a very professional clinic — I am happy about that part — and her roommate stayed with her all day.

We spoke on the phone, had a ceremony when she came back. It was best for us, and what seemed like, the world. But it is undeniable: like Eve, women have the short end of this unavoidable temptation. Don't expect fairness or equal burden. When it comes to reproduction, there are definitely things worth talking about and even requiring on exams before placing diplomas on those all too eager heads. Ounces of prevention, pounds of cure.

* * *

"Can't repeat the past? Why, of course you can." This is the capstone of Jay Gatz' fantasy about how life works. And we understand, most of us, how unrealistic this is. But what if he had said "Can't *change* the past? Why, of course you can." How much more seriously would we have taken his project? Because, in point of fact, there is one way to change the past; especially if you are an educator, counselor, doctor, minister, politician or anyone in direct service to people. One sure way to erase 10, 20, or even 30 years of your life. Get caught in a sexual relationship: the odder, less acceptable to society, the more completely you can change your past.

Post-liaison, whether in jail or not, you are no longer the same person who rendered service all those years. You become a menace who stalked the building, preying on innocents or at least manipulating those you had power over. Any good you may have accomplished is wiped away; all the people you helped retrieve any trust or good-will. This is more than a mistake; it's a solemn betrayal, high treason, grounds for any amount of sanction or ignominy. Sex, after all, is taboo in the larger social sphere. (In this, at least, my family was not so far from the norm.) Inappropriate sex, especially with those you have authority over or use to satisfy a personal obsession, is doubly taboo. Felons incarcerated because of it are unanimously despised and severely punished by some of the least principled people on the planet: their cell-mates. And if you want to really push buttons, go for trebly taboo, you write a book or present findings that in any way casts doubt or simply asks important questions about these issues.

And please, please (please!) do not mistake any of this as an apology for sexual abuse of any kind, stripe or flavor. "Anything goes" sexual wrongs never went well, especially in the '60s and '70s. They are clearly dishonest, universally deceitful, justifiably illegal, spiritually bankrupt, and, (hello?!) still happen with some frequency. The gym teacher, the psychologist, the minister or priest. It is excruciatingly sick to take advantage of people who need your help: narcissism elevated to a religion.

But because sex is a fundamental human need, it stands to reason there will be sexual charges present in the relationships which working with people entail, and that some will fall to this pull.

This is particularly loathsome to suggest in regards to children because it taps into deep-rooted instincts to protect them from harm; and also, I honestly believe, because we don't like to consider children as being fully human. They are somewhere between a miracle creation, a chunk of our being, a developing family-member, an infinite vessel for hopes, dreams and fears, and other things too — but decidedly not an autonomous person, fully independent of our control and authority. As such, the thought of their sexuality tangles hopelessly in our own urge to surrender to this need, tripping alarms and blowing circuits, forcing us into sordid encounters we would just as soon live without. Our own fear, misunderstanding and denial of sexuality propels us into reaction, into rejecting such acts as barbarous, unimaginable, inhuman. That's why anyone who violates this sexual symbiosis, or even suggests it, deserves to lose everything in our estimation: their livelihood, freedom, and especially their past as a member of the human family.

In St. Cloud, my sister was in the theater group at Apollo High School in the '70s. It stuns me today to think about it, but we all knew the director at the high school was seducing the leads. Like the senior girl down the block who, in my 9th grade estimation, was remarkably pretty and talented, her heels clicking signals as she walked to and from the bus drops. This guy never got my sister, even though she was the lead in *Brigadoon* (he did try), but he did a lot of other high school girls up in the sound booth or wherever he could until he got caught and the scandal grew to state-wide proportions. The thing is that this was common knowledge, or, at least seemed to be back then, but somehow was also considered private, nothing to worry about, none of our business. Sex was not discussed and illicit sex, while drawing smirks, was not on the radar screen. In Vermont, after graduation from high school, I learned from one of my friends whom I considered to be straight-laced and prim that she was having an affair with an English teacher. My provincial mind was shocked. Shocked! The "just cause" of the '60s had transmogrified into the "just 'cause" of the '70s right under my nose.

In a high school where I taught for many years, we had a basketball coach-gym teacher type whose reputation was less than sterling. Typically, late on game-nights, past midnight, there were still two cars in the parking lot: his and the team "manager," invariably an attractive senior willing to help with the books, equipment and incidentals behind locked doors, down in the coach's office, after all the statistics were in. He was handsome: tall, blondish, personable and deft, just past 40, but still youthful in his body. I still remember the Friday afternoon when the assistant principal came over the P.A., asking him to report to the office immediately. In retrospect, the voice sounded tense: called down, like a bad boy to face the music. I saw him walking from the building the last time with a gym bag and a basketball under his arm, from behind at least, looking deflated.

On Monday afternoon, there was a special meeting called: mandatory. Everyone filed in quietly, realizing the district office people were down front with serious faces. The assistant principal dutifully checked off names at the door. The personnel director, in charge of more than 1,000 district employees, steps up and begins: "I know you have all heard rumors about an inappropriate relationship between one of our faculty members and a student. I'm here to present what we know, what we can reveal and also to ask for cooperation. First, let me say, that this is the sickest, most disgustingly perverse, twisted sexual encounter that I have ever heard about in a school setting, and I don't want you to breathe a word about it!" My ears pricked up. Like everyone, I thought: "How terrible. What *precisely* did they do?"

Rumors were flying, though, of course, the only people who knew anything were kids. It seems they had this gym teacher red-handed: the team manager was in the hospital with depression and complications from bulimia; she had spilled the beans to her friend, who went directly to parents. They had receipts from restaurants and motels, incriminating notes; panties were somehow involved, along with graphic articles and highlighted paragraphs. Yes, it was sick, and so was the girl: her parents divorced, self-esteem a puddle, her life and reputation in tatters. The whole sordid mess was fully as bad as Mr. Personnel made it seem, and now thanks to him, twice as interesting to talk about. The school district pleaded ignorance — even though they did or should have known — washing their hands of a bad apple. The coach got off light; the girl was 18: no jail time, lost a pension, his license, his job and his home. He moved to Nebraska with his wife and kids and does construction — for all I know, building schools.

You read accounts about similar incidents at least a couple times a year, the most publicized ones involving women professionals with underage male victims. And with the Catholic Church reeling from widespread pedophilia, there is renewed interest in keeping children safe, as well as establishing the "profile" of abusers. A union official spoke to our faculty after the case became public, painting a picture of the typical teacher who goes down for cause: Male, over 40, 20-plus years of experience, well-respected and successful. The suggestion was, with more power and authority, one acquires a propensity for misusing it.

Likely, there is no set pattern to sexual abuse of minors and certainly none for sexual liaisons on the job, but I think it is at least useful to acknowledge two broad realms of accountability: one individual, the other institutional.

With individuals, the fact that abuse tends to occur as perpetrators acquire more authority confirms that power does corrupt, and absolute power corrupts absolutely. This is a predicament because the most effective, compelling and successful professionals are usually those with experience. Apparently, as the ego becomes acquainted with success, humility and sensitivity for the work's mission, as well as the fragile humanity in victims, declines. People become inured, take things for granted, lose touch with original circumstances and intentions. The mind is fooled into believing that "This is O.K; this is justifiable," even when it never really is.

This happens, probably, little by little, one rationalization at a time: "I am helping this person understand something." "It's O.K. for us to be close." "Perhaps I can show them, teach them, how relationship/sexuality works." "I'm not hurting anyone." "No one will find out." "Just this once." Such self-justifying talk follows the route traveled by alcoholics, drug-users, convicts and all those trapped in a cycle of narcissistic need. Many perpetrators were not bad people to begin with, but, over time, without personal growth, a spiritual practice, honest and sincere relationships — where they discuss feelings, fears, sexuality — they became bad, selfish, incapable of higher ground. Their process led downhill to actions that are irredeemably bad, and they lose everything, even parts of their life which were once good, maybe exceptionally so.

But as important, accountability must be shared by the social institution involved. In my experience, they frequently ignore, overlook and discount sexual matters, provide few safeguards and little training to avoid it, and do almost nothing to address the damage inflicted on victims. Individual actions are always mediated by some sense of social propriety and acceptance, even if we just want to "stick a finger in their eye," react against "them." The individual balances decisions with understanding, however ill-informed, of what society — or at least those who matter most

— will make of it. The Colombine killers, committing one of the most anti-social acts in American history, talked repeatedly about how society would view their assault, particularly their moms and dads. The '60s "movement" as such, was largely a self-conscious attempt to install new social values and priorities for ones which had been perceived to fail. We depend on organizations, institutions, religions and even families to fortify an individual's ethical behavior, inoculate them against dark excesses calling from off the garden path.

In this sense, the failings of the Catholic clergy speak volumes about decay within the Church — and Colombine volumes about the rotten core of suburban America. Priests fully understood that molestation was wrong not only from a spiritual point-of-view, or illegal from a societal perspective, but that their entire community, having educated and inculcated them, would be wounded, wronged, and potentially mortally debased by their crimes. Yet, this was not enough. When an individual bites — even rips at — the hand that feeds it, there is indeed something rotten in Denmark. Codes and norms, as constructed through human relationship in myriad organizations, fail. Either, in the words of W.B. Yeats, "the center cannot hold" human company together, our institutions are incapable of winning hearts and minds, or else this sexuality thing is a tad bigger than we realize.

* * *

I once heard Jacob Bronowski, creator of the brilliant *Ascent of Man* series on PBS, suggest that there is no greater profligacy in nature than a man's ejection of several million sperm cells during coitus — with only one being biologically necessary to create life. In plain terms, nature came to evolution by stacking odds in her favor; we are hardwired to fruitfulness and multiplying (despite any additional urging from God). Bronowski also said: The human species is the only one that mates face-to-face, with the female as capable of orgasm as the male, thus making the process not only an instrument of pleasure but of "mutuality." Mutuality. That seems central to a healthy relationship — a sure way to ground charges of sexual energy — but it is not often heard in America's pop culture and certainly not around school.

Bronowski did not discuss, as far as I know, how we are the only species to write compendiums about different positions by which to mate, create vast financial empires — exploiting large numbers of women and children — titillating fellow species members about mating, make endless veiled suggestions about it in media, and then ask youngsters, ones with the perfect bodies for it, to deny, ignore and discount what adults are so busy treasuring. It may be useful to admit that we are dealing with a force here — sexuality, evolution, the survival instinct — that is much greater than ourselves or our ability to understand and control. It tricks and treats us regularly. Our ability to handle it responsibly and with dignity as a mass culture seems to slip more every year.

As such, each of us is probably destined to fail to some degree, even if only by "lusting in our heart" like Jimmy Carter, as our mind considers how it can selflessly — or selfishly — work out these inborn entanglements. Like any life-long process, there will be moments of wisdom, years of muddling through to decency, perhaps a few less than innocent mistakes in which our weakness or deceitful voice talks us into something we can't be proud of. At least, that's what happened to me. There is no sure antidote against failing, though strong institutions, vital and open relationships, as well as clear and explicit information, are the best preventative measures. I know that, more than anything, I needed to talk with an adult during the time of Sarah's pregnancy; find a guide to show me a responsible path forward. Perhaps better curriculum, a dynamic instructor or speaker, and realistic discussions with peers would have helped too.

The same is true for all youngsters struggling to understand sexuality, to perform as fully developed human beings. There is no substitute for dynamic, loving connection with peers and adults, or honest discussions that hold the body up for reverence and the miracle it is. Invariably, we turn up better results with a healthy mix of human interaction and quality information. A pledge of abstinence made under the guise of a parent's wish, a religion's wisdom or even just an individual's best intention, may or may not last until honeymoon (though advocates believe any sexual delay is grounds for celebration). But hard questions remain: What will ensure that the later-to-be adult's sexuality will be appropriately conceived and expressed? Potential addictions curbed? Sexual relationships healthy and happy over the long term?

If anything is true about life, it is to expect change. Taking "the pledge" is an attempt to fix a point and compel constellations to revolve around it; but the likelihood of its steadfastness, and especially its long-term efficacy, is dubious. Priests and professionals in all fields are taught to say "no," to deny themselves and their feelings at all costs. Their markers are out there for years. Some of them deny themselves so much that when they give up believing in decency, group norms, the ethic of community — turning in on themselves and their impulses — a new but related form of denial kicks in: one which sees nothing particularly wrong with certain actions. Denial breeds more denial.

It makes more sense that young people head out into that brave new world beyond the sun and moon with the best charts, understanding and personal lamp-bearers they can muster. They want and need to know that there is a broadly conceived path through the thick parts of becoming a sexual being — plenty of available resources and help. And also, that family and friends care that they are safe, happy and keep in vital touch about what is going on. Care breeds more care. And, healthier relationships. We need to teach kids not just to say "no," but to seek the eyes of their partner as they think about saying "yes." To ask honest questions of each other and themselves; to listen if this is really good for them both, for that mutual and profoundly complicated relationship they are trying to structure around love.

* * *

In the summer of my 8th grade year, I committed a felony. The situation was this: myself, Jack Danielson and Brian Loncar were curious about marijuana. Danielson was my best friend. He lived a couple blocks away with his intriguing parents, a matronly librarian and an owlish bureaucrat, his older siblings already out of the nest. One of his brothers, the most admired, was a detective in Alaska and odd yarns of wilderness, crime and technology found their way into our conversation. Jack was a good spitter, too. Beneath wavy brown hair, he could eject saliva in a half-dozen different ways, each of them top-notch, though they all stood for the same thing: Danielson, decisive as a man. A young man for sure, but one with detective in his blood and no small access to savoir-faire.

Admittedly, he didn't know much about pot, except that it was popular in the older crowd and a kid named Donovan had some growing outside his window near Rigsby's farm. I knew Donovan only slightly. He and another boy had initiated me into junior high by making me push a penny with my nose, hands behind my back, along the walk in front of our house. What they didn't tell you was that while you pushed, they might grab your legs and elevate your torso, nose first along the concrete, scraping skin off your snout. Donovan also failed to mention that being initiated did not exempt you from later proceedings by similar guilds within the school. (In fact, Danielson and I ended up getting initiated a second time, dragged while screaming "Donovan already got us" and thrown under the drama stage by 8th grade louts at the end of football practice.)

We showed up at Donovan's early one August morning with the idea of retribution, though, for me, fear was the dominant emotion. The Donovan house was not on a street, nor was it a farm exactly. A dirt road led back through a clearing to a Tudor-style dwelling that fought off wilderness with a white fence and some broken sidewalk leading exactly nowhere. We were no pros, but it didn't take long to find what we came for, a plant almost twice our size with the habit of a Christmas tree. We snuck in through the gate up to the house where I could see in through a screen. Anybody might be in there, Donovan, his brother, the old man — rumored to give vicious beatings to his boys. Hopefully they were gone, though you couldn't tell from the cars caked around their lot.

Two of us pulled and got the plant up by the roots when, suddenly, a dog starts to bark; by the sound of it, not a wimpy dog. We ran like hell, watering the garden down our pant-legs. These are the moments that predict basic success or failure much more accurately than standardized tests: running for your life, marijuana over your shoulder, pursued by vigilantes with a full range of motorized vehicles and no compunction about blood or cruelty. I passed all right, sprinting up the trail junction ahead of Danielson and Loncar, slowing only much later, as they called to me. I was either a hell of an athlete or one terrified chicken-shit.

That afternoon we tried our darndest to smoke the leaves from a pipe that Danielson got from his father's collection; nothing but a raunchy throat and headache came from it. That might have been the end, except we tried again the next day with drier leaves. This time there was action. I'm not sure I can do it justice, but after a period my mind lapsed into a kind of imagistic spooling through childhood. Certain patterns played over and over: my first crib, bedroom wallpaper, odd passages in our old house. Rhythmic, precisely sequenced, it was like an avant-garde film taking me through a tour of infancy. I sat there and rocked, head in my lap, Danielson keeping me tethered.

At one point we could hear Loncar in the distance calling out, looking for us, but that just made me laugh. Neither of us liked him that much. He was out there, a voice fading away, and we were secure in a copse of bushes. It seemed hilarious. Laughing, I traveled inward and outward, experienced tremendous mental and imagistic tumult over a couple hours, then came down to the physical needs of water and company and food. I had gotten high. There was no money or dealing, no scars or addiction, but in some real sense I understood I had crossed a Rubicon. Donovan's plant had sent me way out there, and also yielded as much as an ounce — in places a felony — which Danielson and I split that night because by morning, my family was winging on its way with all our possessions to far-off Minnesota.

* * *

I am not making the case that marijuana is good for people (though it does seem to help sick patients) or that kids should be allowed to freely have sex; in fact, I don't advocate either to those under 18. But neither do I believe they are inherently bad or evil. In fact, I consider that each has played an important role in allowing me to grow into a real person: someone who's experienced both high and low, felt winging excitement as well as plummeting anguish. If that makes me criminal or deviant in the eyes of society, so be it; but I am not a dreadful person. Neither are the legions of baby-boomers in whose footsteps I followed, nor young adults today experimenting with pot or learning about sex in America's basements and garages. These are not criminals, mug shots of losers and thugs, but children, raised in our culture, trying to find themselves in a confusing and confused environment.

What we are really doing with our obsession over marijuana is making young people out to be bad — insisting that if they step across a line, they will taste the full measure of "badness" as instituted by authorities with guns, handcuffs and badges. Evil is not lurking here, but behavior you should expect in a consumer society whose principal virtue is freedom and whose chief vice is a need for pleasure. There is no credible reason why two marijuana seeds on the carpet of a student's car should result in their expulsion from high school. Nor for regular and random drug-testing of students during normal school hours. Nor for school drug raids with German Shepherds and weapons drawn. Nor for stripping federal loan assistance from kids who have at some point in the past been convicted of a marijuana violation. Nor for a thousand other official school or government policies, petty and profound in their message about what kind of culture we really are. The really "bad" people in all this are the ones who believe that because youngsters are not yet legal adults, their rights can be trampled, due-process compromised, a future thrown away.

There is a kind of McCarthyism behind America's Drug War, the elevation of social distrust into an end itself. As if contact with a banned substance/information/attitude is enough to corrupt your entire soul, make you less than human and therefore, like sexual impropriety, justifies any level of government intrusion and punishment. I understand that drugs are dangerous; dangerous to those who use and abuse, and also to society which must clean up the mess. My argument here is only in regards to marijuana, that '60s icon which is proving less toxic, physically addictive, and more therapeutic than realized, and which both Canada and England have recently moved to decriminalize. I am not wholly an innocent; I have battle-scars and wounds in this too. Alcoholism and addiction run in my family, in my blood. The journal I have from high school reads like one long plea for help: to stop smoking so much pot, to limit the cycle of drinking and revelry associated with my circle of friends.

And I hurt more than myself. When I was a junior in high school, I drove my younger brother John to a cinema in Burlington — some fantasy science-fiction flick with wizards and dragons, remarkable because it was the first time he ever smoked dope. He was 14, a scrawny freshman. I remember as an infant that he had casts on his legs to correct a leg irregularity. He used to pound these on the floor or table as he lay strapped in his baby seat, "Bam-Bam-Bam," as if he knew what was coming and wanted out. He grew up loving the outdoors, throwing sticks as spears with his strengthening left arm, making an impressive bellowing roar in imitation of a bear. We swam, we hiked, we played football. I knew his strong little body better than anyone from wrestling holds, tackles and races we ran.

This was John as I remember him that night. Afterward, I'm not sure I knew him again. The look on his face is frozen in memory: a bleary, confused wonderment, unearthly in the spell it held on him, eyes lacking course as if tossed on an ocean of lolling waves. He and his buddy limped into the cold, pulled their pants, headed for a film experience which mesmerized them for all time. Unfortunately, too, an experience that John sought to recapture again and again in high school and beyond, using beer, liquor, hashish, even cocaine as he got older. After that night, we went on to perfect the suburban adolescent party chamber: every school night another opportunity to do bongs, cruise back roads sniggering, listen to tunes, come home, munch out and play backgammon in front of T.V.

The sad facts boil down to this. My brother became an addict, at one point able to drink almost a liter of liquor a day. He got caught up in cocaine, smoked crack, blacked out in sprees of all-night partying, crashed his car, got busted, did treatment, ditched his halfway-house and recovery program, went on the lam, continued to abuse, did treatment again, regressed, recovered. My brother, my baby brother whose face said, "I'm innocent," whose life was supposed to be mine to help steer, slipped through fingers into the hell of dependency and I couldn't, or didn't, do much to prevent it. I visited him in treatment the first time; and the second. I remember one spring in my mid-20s, when I was safely in a 12-step group, crying underneath a flowering Japanese plum tree in my yard. White sweet-smelling blossoms fell gently around me making it seem like winter in the isolation of my grief. Every year, white petals remind me of those first tears, our family's deep wounds. I do not cry easily.

* * *

Drugs are not glamorous or wonderful as frequently portrayed in pop culture, particularly because we rarely see the downside of dependency. Addiction is the bane of individual freedom — its diabolical twin — and from the very first work of literature in the Western World, *The Odyssey*, we are shown the dangers of dependency or any seduction away from the goal of making it "home" — the Ithaca in all of us. It is an old story; one not about to change. Nothing is more baleful or heartrending than alcoholism or addiction to narcotics, temptations that push us further out into the sea of alone. In our effort to prevent drug and alcohol abuse, I want to suggest that we have lost perspective about what we are fighting and why. As a member of the National Rifle Association might say if ever committed to treatment: "Drugs don't abuse people; people do." We are killing the messenger in our attempt to stop the undesirable effects of drugs, but allow the message to be ignored, time and again, only to do more damage. We freely allow guns but find the effects of drugs beyond the pale. The real message should be about people doing the abuse, not their instrument of destruction. Their pain and the way they kill it varies from person to person, but it is nonetheless a deeper truth that the distress of despair, of hurt, of no love is what drives addiction.

We have legal ways to express it — through pornography, alcohol, gambling, even work and sports; and we have ways that, in our wisdom, we have consigned to illegality — drugs, some aspects of sex, and some forms of gambling. To think that the dividing line we draw through these dependencies is rational or fair is to live in the same ignorance I believed in as a child, oblivious to my parent's sexual appetites. The naked truth is that the needs of an average human often strain the edges of social decency; even more so under the rubric of large-scale freedom and end-less opportunities to play and consume. Only relationship — relationship with people, relationship with God or art or working out — can keep the majority of us from going over the line. The formula is far simpler than we imagine, and needs only an early start and consistent mention right up through high school to be effective: Care breeds more care — and healthier relationships.

Now close your eyes. Imagine being a child today. One without self-confidence, a loving family or effective teachers. Imagine trying to navigate your way through a jungle of attraction and exclusion, needing to fit in, following the impulse to be new and unique, looking for guides while being asked to consume more and far better than your peers. Imagine that you have nothing to lose by taking chances, that all you want is to escape the place and people assigned to you; maybe even to escape yourself. Now open your eyes: what young people really need are good friends, a place to hang out and a society which encourages their uniqueness and belief in a decent future.

* * *

The war over the legacy of the '60s and '70s continues in the way we handle sex and drugs and also to an extent, rock n' roll. My throw-away line about journals — *No sex, no drugs, no rock 'n roll* — is more prescient than I ever realized. Stacked up against the war on terrorism, the need for a clear head and fair policies at home is more important than ever. How long will we continue to believe that ignorance of our sexual nature is going to promote healthy relationships in an environment of explosive sexual fascination? How much longer will we spend time and resources locking citizens away whose only crime was to grow a native plant? When will we "dare" acknowledge that with millions experimenting with sex or smoking pot every day, current programs and emphases are neither effective, appropriate, nor sustainable in a nation that believes in democracy, freedom and human rights?

And the issue really is about freedom. America is supposed to be a place that allows citizens free reign to create that which proves liberty's mettle and worth. Our credo espouses freedom as the foundation for achievement, innovation and continuous advancement. It asserts that in allowing choice and trusting instincts of free people, our nation is propelled forward — socially, economically, spiritually. Contained in that ethos is agreement that "free choice" is the irreducible core — choice that sometimes turns out badly, but which should never be pre-empted or determined by others, and certainly not by authorities or institutions. In a free country, there must always exist the possibility of mistakes, whether on state-sponsored exams or in the methods chosen to pursue happiness. However appalling or inconvenient, the privilege to err must be defended as the most basic of human rights.

In a way, a big way actually, America is the one to have let the freedom genie out of the bottle — it is a singular contribution to humanity — and we have conjured its magic to propel an economic and political agenda across five continents. On the surface, our program calls for democracy, transparency, open markets, individual rights and liberty, but the blunt instruments we use to insert these overmaster the good intentions we may have had — if we had any to begin with. Large scale capitalism has no basis in morality or human ethics, and precious little sensitivity for local culture. Like sex, there is no talk about "mutuality": America is strong, the other an underling. Yet a majority of Americans continue to support this uncritically, conflating it with America's ideology that people around the world must have the same essential yearning as we do: to be free.

It is inevitable that the curtain gets lifted on America's huffing and puffing about freedom. After California voted to allow medical marijuana for suffering patients, the federal government stepped in to threaten doctors, arrest growers and aggressively break up local dispensaries. In parts of the U.S., drug testing is mandatory and students suspected of using pot or even just possessing paraphernalia are expelled. Meanwhile, the Department of Education is looking at ways it can reward schools for instituting abstinence-only classes where "no" is the essential curriculum. Official fear about an acrid weed and squeamishness over the bodily desires of youth culture — twin icons of the '60s — are compelling author-ities to try to force the genie back in. Good people are being imprisoned, young students left to themselves amidst legal and illegal temptation, disenfranchised foreigners asked to believe our words, ignore our actions. Our choices — how to live and what to believe — are being constrained and constricted into ever narrower channels of official acceptability.

It has been correctly pointed out that America is increasingly divided against itself in a "culture war." But it has not been frequently mentioned that only one side has the full weight and authority of government to impose its views on the other, deathly afraid that any admission of fallibil-ity or mistakes in official policy will return us to the turmoil of decades past. Thus the '60s continue to haunt and influence as never before. The machinery of an intrusive state-sponsored morality has been erected to suppress and control things about freedom we don't like, our own people not trusted to find their way to responsible, independent lives. And public school — the young people as always — is the central battle-ground for this unwise and unwinnable imperative.

brown vs. the board

"Oh beautiful
For spacious skies
For amber waves of grain.
For purple mountains majesty
Above the fruited plain.

"America, America
God shed his grace on thee
And crowned thy good with brotherhood
From sea to shining sea."

We sang this around the flagpole in 5th grade at Madison Elementary in St. Cloud. I was in Mrs. White's class with 20 other 12-year-olds, and because it was a windy day and cold, holding hands seemed more palatable than potentially getting the "cooties" from Loralee Lewis — which by now every boy had by virtue of our unbroken circle. No doubt there was jostling and wisecracks, but no one was going to try Mrs. White that morning: her formal coat and determined look meant no funny business. The flag's rusty chain clattered against the aluminum pole beneath Old Glory making a discordant harmony to our song which we had not rehearsed.

Mrs. White, tall and full-figured in my memory, dressed crisply in blouses or sweaters over suitably professional skirts and projected an air of knowing competence in all matters. (Even when she pronounced the word "caribou" as "cari-bow-a," which because of *Mutual of Omaha's Wild Kingdom* I knew was not right.) She wore thick-rimmed glasses of those times but was not considered unattractive amongst us boys, who proved maturity by discussing such things. When she came up in kickball, we ran on our little legs to the deepest corners of the playground because we understood that even in skirt and heels, Mrs. White could kick like a mule. Our confidence in her was such that if she told us to stand at attention and sing, we stood and sang. And on this particular morning to honor an American who had recently died after years of service to his country.

Looking around the circle I knew faces and stories of classmates. Not all were friends but in a small town you knew everyone without ever being conscious of having met them. Stevie Campana, glasses held together with medical tape, wore blue hand-me-down pants of brothers who attended St. Peter's. Mary Teneste, child of a doctor, excelled at ballet and piano and would definitely solo if we asked. Dale Pogamon, tallish, mop of red hair, looked like "Lil Abner" and stayed after for math. Stephanie Thomas, on the heavy side, probably enjoyed holding hands more than anyone. Jeff Horton, a new kid from Milwaukee, stood dutifully on call for his country. Dianne Schmitz, who regularly beat me at the 600-yard dash, seemed like a sixth-grader even though she rarely spoke up in class. Jane Erpelding, petite, blond, blue eyes, whom I tried to impress around the monkey bars, held next to me.

We were a pretty typical 5th grade class and considered ourselves normal in every respect, eventually becoming secretaries, musicians and housewives, soldiers, hairdressers and husbands. Descended from Poles, Slavs, Germans and assorted European ethnicities, our unambiguous normality, from this distance at least, seems like our essential weakness: no one was not white and thus able to imagine what that endless clattering beneath the American flag might be insinuating. None of us were Black, Hispanic, Jewish, Asian, nor, except for the Gross family that lived three blocks away and sent children to St. Peter's, Native American. No one considered this troubling; children are usually the last to think in terms of skin color or ethnic difference, even if it presents itself to an astonishing degree. We were good Americans in that regard, standing to honor the life of J. Edgar Hoover who had been the distinguished head of the F.B.I. for more than 35 years.

It may seem odd that an FBI director in Washington should garner so much respect and attention, especially from 5th graders in a far flung province, but J. Edgar Hoover was a powerful man. In many ways more formidable than presidents in his era, he certainly outmaneuvered, outlived, and out-cheated many of them. He became a household name where I grew up — we were a political family — invoked when we conducted neighborhood operations. (If someone got out of line, we threatened to hand their name over to Hoover.) But as we know now with the benefit of documents and hearings, Mr. Hoover was a deeply paradoxical man, violating rights and freedoms of American citizens with impunity. He intimidated judges, blackmailed Congressmen and presided over some ugly chapters in American history, Japanese internment, McCarthyism, the civil rights movement, employing "any means necessary" to subdue what he felt were threats to American security or affronts to his personal power.

He also apparently lived a deeply paradoxical personal life, one that included unusual cross-dressing, adventurous men and scenarios that are the equal to today's best homoerotic films. Very few Americans knew of his contradictory double-life or double-dealings, and certainly no child around the flagpole had a clue about any of this. For my part, with a healthy interest in Jane Erpelding and the prospect of Prison Dodge Ball after lunch, like every one else, I was not unwilling to stand through a civil ceremony for just about anyone.

Looking back now, this small episode speaks volumes to me in regard to America's schools and our understanding of United States' history. As students, we are bombarded with events, stories and qualities which make us a worthy nation. We are taught how George Washington never lied, Lincoln gave his life to fight slavery, F.D.R. rallied us from a wheel-chair to defeat fascism. We stand at mute attention for "The Star Spangled Banner," dutifully recite "The Pledge of Allegiance" and sing out-loud "God Bless America." But we are not taught-and should be — about the skeletons in our American closet: issues whose troubling shadows we prefer to evade, ignore and forget. Reconciling these two aspects of America, our great virtues and our substantial vices, what might be called our "paradoxical nature", is a very thorny personal challenge for me, and within public school perhaps the most neglected dilemma we face as a nation.

* * *

Just as in the song we sang that day, "*America, America*", there are two Americas, but they do not mean the same thing, are not equal, and not even remotely similar. Nor are they crowned by "brotherhood." These two Americas have existed side-by-contradictory-side since the idea of freedom gave birth to our Republic, and they will last as long as a clear majority believes there is only one America, that its story is relatively simple, clear and told in a single voice. Our paradoxical identity as a nation is a chasm that runs like an open wound "from sea to shining sea." It is as plain as black and white, as grotesque as the gulf between the very rich and very poor, and as complex as the divide between actual events and the idealized lenses most Americans view them with.

One America is a version my 5th grade class learned — "shining city on a hill," egalitarian promised land, pulsing giant of industry — drawing people the world over hoping for freedom, a new beginning, a chance to realize their deepest dream. An America where pioneers tamed a harsh land, farmers created the "breadbasket of the world," immigrants pulled themselves up "by the bootstraps," went "west young man" and created "the greatest nation the world has ever known." Hero after hero, mostly white and predominantly male, Paul Revere, Lewis and Clark, Davy Crockett, Daniel Boone, George Custer and many others, real or imagined, inspired this spirit of individuality, hard work and self-reliance. This America is portrayed as a land of "freedom and justice for all," a country that opens its arms to the destitute and forlorn, "hitches its wagon to a star" and never pauses to take a good look back to its origins.

If it had, it may have noticed another America, the one trailing in the dust. The America that did not come here for freedom but arrived in bondage, never to see home or kin again, destined to generations of agony, hard labor and discrimination at the hands of whites. A nation of hardy immigrants that decimated a culture living according to its tradition and which had, more often than not, provided settlers vital assistance. A country to which people came in search of religious freedom, only to end up prosecuting, jailing and sometimes hanging those it suspected of beliefs different than their own. An America which ruined watersheds, burned prairies, logged forests, mined mountains, and nearly extinguished its most respected animals — the wolf, grizzly bear, eagle and buffalo. This is the "*Other America*" of Michael Harrington, of rural and urban poor, of "separate and unequal" schools, of workers exposed to hazardous conditions while earning minimal wages. This America is not ideal because it is sad, disturbing, and violative of our most basic principles. It does not fit our noble image, is infrequently discussed, rarely written about and is completely invisible at sporting events or shopping malls, even though it has existed side-by-contradictory-side with America the First. In its simplest and most paradoxical form, it is an America which has experienced our nation's great freedom, not as a celebrated privilege but as an imposing misery.

This reality, of there being two Americas, is not an original idea: academics, historians, philosophers, and now, because of John Edwards, even politicians have acknowledged it over decades. Simply to be black or brown or poor or even a woman is enough to understand its import. What I am trying to surface is how this issue has yet to penetrate classrooms as a matter of regular study and discussion. And also, how pressing the reality of there being two Americas has become; thus, how the need to confront it directly has grown. What I am speaking about — our paradoxical nature — is not restricted to race, though that may be its most identifiable divide. It is not limited to wealth, though that may be its most impenetrable weakness. And it is not principally a question of mistakes out of history, though most Americans may prefer to see it that way. Our dual nature, of being at once a wonderfully skilled, responsive and advanced nation, and at times painfully myopic, unfeeling and bungling, is persistent, real and very much a contemporary phenomenon. It is as much a framework for seeing what happens today as it is a prism to analyze our past.

* * *

An organization called the *Council on Public Diplomacy* reported in its 2002 survey that a striking majority of people in other nations, friend and foe, regard America as being "arrogant, self-absorbed and self-serving" amongst other pejoratives. Their findings were widespread and unusually uniform. (This was prior to our internationally unpopular military campaign in Iraq in 2003.) The reaction of most Americans who read or heard about the report was shock and surprise. There were immediate calls, and legislation providing actual dollars, to hire public relations firms to get our story out to these other countries, many of them important allies. Programs are now up and running, with radio stations, commercials and features carefully placed in foreign media to offset this negative impression.

Unfortunately, there can be no hiding or talking our way around some of the most basic facts as perceived by other parts of the world. Their conceptions about us may be selective, shorn from context and freighted with prejudice, but they do, nonetheless, have elements of truth. Only one nation has utilized nuclear weapons against civilians in the midst of hostilities. Only one country loudly trumpets the virtues of freedom while locking up more people per capita than anyone else. One well-to-do nation has the biggest Gross Domestic Product, greatest number of business start-ups and most flexible labor markets, but also an alarming disparity between rich and poor and higher rates of poverty, infant mortality, homicide and HIV infection, at least among similarly industrialized peers. One developed country spends more than all others on medical care yet leaves tens of millions without regular access to health services, under-serving its most vulnerable people — the old, the sick and the young. One wealthy state spends billions on weapons of mass destruction — biological, chemical, nuclear — rejects most attempts to ban or control them through international treaty, then calls other countries who pursue such policies "rogue nations" and "terrorist states."

Meanwhile, this same democracy trains a large, well-armed force to detain, arrest, and all too frequently kill its most troubled and marginal citizens using the motto "to serve and protect." Gun deaths in America exceed those of all other developed nations combined. Energy consumption in percentage terms is five times greater than our population. Our lack of credibility with the rest of the world is not simply a matter of making a better presentation or rubbing shoulders with the right journalists over cocktails. It is the result of what we have done and continue to do at home and abroad, and how these stories — this history — reverberate in the minds of people watching us. They see something other than what we propose for ourselves. Another instance of there being two Americas.

My point is not to bash the United States, a land I cherish and respect, to which my ancestors gladly came and worked hard to shape. My purpose is to raise the honesty with which we discuss our history and conditions: to present our dual nature fairly in education so that another generation starts a little further ahead confronting the problems which confound us. The question is this basic: In a very busy and highly managed school environment, where accountability through standardized tests is the only measure of success and textbooks are carefully picked by committees beholden to conservative interests, which stories about American history or our contemporary circumstances will be presented to students? Will we fairly represent the virtuous aspects of America side-by-side with our notable short-comings? Will we, in short, take the time — and the pains — to admit that there are two Americas and always have been?

Consider how problematic is the story of Thomas Jefferson, one of our most accomplished public servants. We have always known (though never emphasized) that while writing the *Declaration of Independence*, around 200 black men, women and children labored to improve Monticello as slaves. People love the majesty of Monticello, its gardens and buildings, but rarely acknowledge the system that allowed him to build such an estate in the first place. We also know that Mr. Jefferson would not have been elected had not blacks in the south counted as three-fifths of a person (though ineligible to vote), thus giving Jefferson the electoral majority he needed to win. Further, as one version would have it — and it is supported by DNA evidence — Mr. Jefferson helped himself to a sexual relationship with Sally Hemmings, a slave, producing children without freedoms that Jefferson's words confer on white citizens, including his own children with his wife.

162

What aspects of Thomas Jefferson's story, and now Sally Hemming's or their children together, do we present in our schoolrooms? Should we continue to ignore and dodge the difficulty of these paradoxical versions of America's legacy? Or is it possible to knit them together into fabric which more fully depicts the wholeness of America's complex experience? I do not have any easy answers or outcomes, but in a nation which says it treasures diversity, open debate and truth, I am willing to ponder questions that need to be confronted — especially in front of the children.

* * *

America is often portrayed as the first country founded not on power or privilege but upon an ideal: the love of freedom. Jefferson believed in it as much as anyone. The basic premise, as received through the Enlightenment, is that when free, human beings reach full potential, utilize their gifts for the greatest good. This is used to explain the United States' meteoric climb to prominence and power, rising like a cork from the depths to world leadership, and generally Americans accept freedom as the unifying basis of our strength. What is rarely mentioned is that freedom does not present individuals with clear moral imperatives or even equip them with distinct ethical strategies. The founders, in their wisdom, left that to religion, civic virtue and private conviction. We hope citizens act responsibly and enact extensive laws to compel it, but basically the (majoritarian) people of the United States are allowed to pursue a way of life that most appeals to them, they have means to afford or that they can get away with. They may move west, assist others, build a homestead and become stewards of the land; or, they may ride into the sunset stealing horses, gambling and drinking themselves to death on gold taken from Reservation lands.

Our political system is built upon checks and balances because the Founding Fathers understood that human nature, as evidenced by human freedom, means that no one person or body can be trusted with exclusive authority. What America has really accomplished is to provide a stage upon which actors from many parts and persuasions are given rein to create whatever suits their taste or private obsession. In the abstract it is true freedom but as it engages with competing values and human nature — maximizing personal pleasure and profit, tapping abundant natural resources, vying for power, using the rationale of "protecting freedom" to wipe out resistance or rivals — it is easy to visualize the essential predicament of our culture: how race was used to exploit, why prisons are overcrowded, why corporations commit abuses, and why a man like J. Edgar Hoover violated the rights of countless American citizens. Through freedom — at least for those lucky enough to obtain the genuine article — this nation provides the right to be truly human, either the best or worst that can mean. People may choose their highest calling; or, they might revert to their lowest. And this is precisely why, from the very first moment of our Republic, there have always been two Americas.

I believe that educating students about United States history should begin with this premise, then proceed to examples from both in our enduring odyssey of taking on an enormous, plentiful, raw, non-white continent. It is not shameful to point out that humans always choose between right and wrong, moral or immoral, compassion or hatred, and that as history went along these terms changed, were refined to include more actions once acceptable or unacceptable but which today are seen differently. Slavery was abolished (largely) because it was seen as inhumane and unworkable; women gained rights (mostly) due to the moral justness of their cause; unions were instituted (generally) because we sought balance to the power of capitalists; diversity is (usually) portrayed as an asset because we understand there are gifts that differences provide. And in all of these cases, there were movements challenging authority, debates which prompted change, laws enacted, but eventually, to America's credit, a new path forged leading freedom and opportunity forward. But none of it was accomplished without resistance or sacrifice, hard work and activism, legal means as well as jail time. We should be justly proud that citizens did die to forge "a more perfect union," not only in wars at home and abroad but also in struggling to right historic wrongs within our own communities.

* * *

Presenting a litany of failings committed under the umbrella of American freedom, whether official government mistakes, communally despicable acts or individual transgressions, is not pleasant, comfortable or unambiguous. Certainly, if Mr. Johnson, our principal at Madison Elementary that day, had gotten on the intercom to announce that J. Edgar Hoover had been a cross-dressing hypocrite who violated fundamental rights of Americans that he had sworn to uphold and protect, there likely would have been calls to the school board and perhaps for Mr. Johnson's resignation. But I doubt there would have been many adults sitting up with their children that night capable of disentangling the whole mess.

What I have been talking about here are paradoxes: two opposing and frightfully contradictory notions which are both true. They are frustrating because they seemingly block clear understanding within the framework of standard logic. How can "A" be "A," but also, at the same time, be "B"? (Especially to officials who believe they measure learning with exams where there is only one answer, and "A" is never other than "A.") How can the United States be one of the biggest perpetrators of environmental pollution and also, because of its science and technology, one of Nature's few hopes for conservation and protection? How can the United States be one of the biggest proponents and defenders of freedom, and at the same time, through corporate globalization and an unrivalled military, one of its biggest threats? How can we have both the freest society and the most people behind bars? How can we have the best medical system and also one of the most inefficient and inaccessible? How can a leader like J. Edgar Hoover, entrusted with defending the highest ideals of our country, also be one of our biggest offenders? The rational powers upon which we depend for clear answers break down as contradictions arise and are not laid to rest.

Paradoxes are troubling, even frustrating; they are also more pervasive than commonly understood. Day flows effortlessly into night with no defining climax or even any perceptible moment-to-moment change. We proceed in our lives — building a career, home and family — as if we will live more or less indefinitely even though our demise is only a single breath away. The most basic elements of nature, sun, water and wind, can appear as either great blessings or terrible natural disasters. One of the oldest teachings from China, the yin-yang symbol, captures the dualistic nature of opposites, how they both combine and even contain each other to some degree. Humans have been given a great power — rational thought — but reality is not constrained to such predictable confines. We perceive paradox because the world is made from it, and that includes ourselves.

Looking back through this book, I see that, quite unintentionally, most chapters hold a paradox which shapes a central issue within it: Growing up at the end of a large family made me feel superfluous, insignificant, which in turn drove me inward, inspired my love of literature and writing. To fully understand the character of America, it is critical to live abroad, appreciate our culture through the eyes of others. Because I had trouble speaking in front of groups, I forced myself into teaching. Educating others is not so much a question of material facts or mastering concepts as it is learning to foster an effective process: assisting students' search for connections between an "out-there" and an "in-here." Teaching in contemporary high school is so packed with paradox, compounded by contradiction, inundated by irony, that most either leave, burn-out or settle into a long cynical stand-off, accepting little jabs and huge frustrations as the price for a stable life-style. Play is both a natural pleasure and release as well as a distraction from important personal and national concerns. Human sexuality can be an expression of deep love and the impetus for our survival as a species or it can become something hideously narcissistic leading to a downfall. In a world that needs and demands certainty — paradox, ambiguity, contradiction — all lead to the same basic place: uncertainty, indecision, ambivalence.

As such, there is not a single answer to paradoxes which confront us, but there is effective thinking and teaching, as well as dignified and humane responses. Parker Palmer, sociologist, educator and erstwhile inspiration for this book, has written about the challenge and reward of remaining open to paradox in *The Courage to Teach*. He speaks of the necessity of taking two opposing views into the heart where reflection, concern for honesty and a desire for truth based upon deep human or religious values can ground them. Real sorrow, a recognition of the immense struggle of the human condition, followed closely by a determination to frame it with compassion is likely the surest way to undo the knot of paradox. As educators, by not fastening our attitude or judgment in place, keeping debate open and extending a willingness to listen and learn, our honesty grows, our understanding of others and their point-of-view deepens. It also models an important attitude and approach for young people: the ability to hear, imagine and understand what life is like for another. (A stark contrast to the political shouting passing as dialogue on radio and television today.) But this only happens if the teacher is fully prepared and equipped for such a possibility; it does not happen by accident. It is not something you acquire by studying, reading or taking notes at a workshop. Being able to fully live out the creative tension in paradox is a condition of being alive; it goes to the core of who you are as a person.

Critics of the so-called "liberal academia" rail against its proclivity to assume the worst about America and her culture, to bludgeon her accomplishments to death with a thousand cuts of criticism. This, along with pressure from parents and a general fear of the unknown, prevents most teachers from pursuing the more challenging aspects of America's past and present. But in reality, more than ever after September 11th, the clarity of our understanding about who we are, as well as our ability to comprehend the bill of goods presented by the world, will determine our ability to survive and thrive as a nation. Our values need to be vigorously questioned and debated in classrooms; our history thoroughly examined, discussed. These are awkward questions but why would we systematically evade or neglect them unless we believe our children — out of fear or guilt — must be sheltered, prevented from seeing struggle or suffering in our past.

Struggle, and particularly suffering are a natural aspect of human existence and history. By embracing their truth we expand the capacity of our heart to endure, not damage some fragile tissue of national identity. I speak from experience when I say that the answers, and most particularly the skills developed through asking the right questions — even if paradoxical — will more than reward us individually and as a nation. Love and respect come cheap when times are good, when we consider the object of our devotion as deserving and triumphant. They are valued more deeply, and more personally, when arrived at after great striving, turmoil and sacrifice. We would be wise as a nation to no longer just cover it up, to tell kids that "we are the greatest nation on earth," while turning the page on racism, closing the book on injustice and intolerance.

* * *

This is not just some pie-in-the-sky wish list for how we could do education better. This is reality in our school buildings now, just as it has always been in educational settings for white and black, rich and poor. It is not easy to explain why America has dedicated an entire month to the study and celebration of black history. Nor is it easy to explain to black students why that month, February, happens to be the shortest of the calendar. Nor is it easy to explain to Asian students or Hispanic or Native Americans why there is not a month to recognize and honor their own heritage.

The upshot to the reaction of Howard University students when the O.J. Simpson verdict was announced surprised no one who understands the difference that accumulates across diverse communities in America. More often than not, despite whatever success a school may have in celebrating and integrating diversity, in diluting the difficulty of there being two Americas, there will always be questions which pull and strain the social fabric, not only in school but across entire communities. The need to recognize and understand that these differences are real and palpable — whether we call them paradoxes or not — is essential to addressing them.

The school where I worked for 10 years, Park Center High School in Brooklyn Park, witnessed a dramatic changeover in clientele from the late 1980s through the turn of the century. Large subsidized apartment complexes were built with government assistance and a sizeable influx of African-American and Asian families migrated there, transforming what had been a typical white post-World War II suburb into a modern day web of diversity. The early years were rough, as percentages of students of color crept from 5 percent toward 20 percent and the teaching staff remained overwhelmingly white. Racial fights and epithets, harassment, hate and fear proliferated despite the tepid attempts by administrators to initiate constructive forums and dialogue.

Even after 10 years, after racial tensions mellowed, after students had grown up with each other from kindergarten through 10th grade, there were still the inevitable disputes arising from such things as a Black History Showcase put on by African-American students. It only takes a single student, however unmotivated or unremarkable, to raise his hand and demand to know when we are going to finally put on a White History Showcase to ignite dormant passions about the fairness of America's racial divide. In a single class period, productive discussions break down along predictable lines, and you hear the language change from "we" and "us", to "they" and "them"; from one school united, to two divided. Suddenly, the innocuous racial divisions in the cafeteria — Whites here, Blacks there, Asians on the side — seem like intractable and ungovernable splits. The reality of two Americas comes into the open for all to see.

Today in this district the reality of two Americas is as apparent as ever. On the east side of the Osseo School District is Park Center, my school, with a facility built in 1972 and remodeled several times to no one's satisfaction. Pacing up its tired courtyard to the front entrance, there are cracks, stains and fissures in the ugly concrete apron. Once inside, you notice the walls of the main three story quad complex are essentially temporary vinyl panels, installed after the completely open floor plan of the early '70s was found to be a poor model for managing hundreds of disinterested adolescents. There is a drop ceiling of white acoustic tile housing washed out fluorescent lighting and poorly functioning mechanical systems; different floors are invariably too hot, too cold or too stuffy. The gym facilities are sub-standard, even for the era in which they were built, with primitive locker rooms and a rubberized tartan-like surface stretched thinly over concrete in the upper gym. Until 2001, there were no football games played on campus because there was no stadium. Bathrooms tend to have shaky plumbing, a single potty stall and are invariably a mess with clogged urinals and sinks and paper towels overflowing the garbage. Drinking fountains are few, far between and frequently out of commission.

Surrounding the school, neighborhoods and housing are as mixed as the student body. Large and dated apartment complexes still stand, some within walking distance to school, attracting recent immigrants and other low-skill urban poor who struggle with basic elements in American life. There is also a sizeable section of small post-War homes, and some more attractive housing built later, with young middle-class families and older, empty nest couples. Local businesses tend to be run-down malls or fraying corporate franchises with aging plants, and the entire civic infrastructure, from roads to sewers to sidewalks is in need of a thorough overhaul. The percentage of students of color at Park Center has mushroomed to over 50 percent, with 36 percent of students qualifying under federal guidelines as being impoverished and 15 percent new learners of English.

In contrast, the very same school district built and opened a new high school in 1996 in Maple Grove, a fast-growing suburb that was only recently rolling hills and farmland. The building was designed using the model of a maple leaf to offer different "houses" within the school, trying to break the impersonal nature of secondary institutions into smaller, more agreeable units. The building features a dramatic two-story atrium, state of the art lighting (which automatically shuts off when no motion is detected in a room) and mechanical systems that really do acclimatize and provide fresh air. There are conference rooms with plush wing seating, wiring for computer displays, full size gymnasiums, ample bathrooms, a huge cafeteria and a state of the art auditorium. It is as nice a facility as could be built for $50 million at the time. To staff it, the district hand-picked applicants from two existing high schools in an effort to create a synergistic educational environment. In short, the finest resources and most effective teachers got shipped to Maple Grove where student enrollment was more affluent, and presumably, more academically motivated.

Maple Grove is a suburb which knows what it wants. In the early '90s, when regional planning authorities suggested balancing their extensive new developments with affordable housing apartments, the community went ballistic, packing meetings, writing angry letters and relentlessly pressuring politicians until the proposal was off the table. Much of the rhetoric from that fight bordered on racism and was clearly a critique of what had happened in Brooklyn Park, where Section 8 housing had made such an impact in a once "lily-white" community. Today, Maple Grove is a series of upscale subdivisions with few, if any, housing options under $350,000. Spiffy new outlet malls with large neon signs and chain restaurants repeat themselves endlessly around a mock town center, all of it accessible only by automobile which means parking lots full to overflowing with giant SUVs. Their high school boasts very high test scores, as well as minority and poverty rates which are miniscule (5 percent and 3 percent respectively), the equal of the most exclusive suburbs in America.

These two schools are immediate neighbors, and in fact depend for funding on the same district administration, Osseo Area Schools, Minnesota's fifth largest. But they might as well be light years apart because by any qualitative or quantitative measure, they occupy different worlds. Even when special State funding was obtained recently to help acculturate immigrants to the realities of America, Maple Grove received almost as much funding as did Park Center. The ironic thing is that when it comes to resources or programs, Maple Grove, with a larger population and a more vocal and well-financed parent network, frequently receives more and better than does Park Center, even if it is Park Center's exploding demographics which attract the funding in the first place. Thus, in a real sense, the rich get richer and the poor, or at least the less successful, get whatever is left. Within this single suburban school district, supported by the same tax base, governed by a (predominantly white) five-member school board and once a quiet homogeneous backwater, it is not hard to miss: there really are two Americas.

* * *

I sometimes wonder why this matters so much to me. I mean, why do I care about racial equality, insist that students share personal stories, openly question school priorities, and especially, write an entire book challenging the status quo in American education? Few of my colleagues seem to notice or fuss much about these issues. Most do their job then go home, and only an occasional parent complains or goes beyond inquiring after specific events involving their child. And while I have tried to paint an accurate portrait of my inner landscape, have accounted for my sensibility in crucial origins and events, it still doesn't add up as to why I believe these things matter so much — view my judgment as somehow better than highly paid, highly educated professionals running the show. Even I have to admit that perhaps none of these things do matter as much as I think. That in the end, it's just not worth the time and effort to remonstrate so intensely about getting it right. That greater America is so immersed in a day-to-day grind that attending to these small and large issues at school is beyond our collective interest, will or attention span.

But somehow, I persist. Not for me, I tell myself, but for the kids. That's why it matters; that's why I stay up late to finish grading, re-work a lesson or struggle so hard to get it right in a book. Where did that come from? I can't be entirely certain, but deep down I sense it's genetic. That like everyone, I began life attached to an umbilical cord, connected to those that made and reared me: my parents, my very first teachers. Their sensibility and values have compelled me to care deeply, imbued within me a sense of pride in my role as educator and advocate. It must be. If the rest of this book has not captured the dogged idealistic core of why this matters so much to me — how I can't turn my back on what I know — then nothing I say now will get us any closer. It's all I know how to do. And I will keep trying regardless. There is something in me, akin to a determined parent, which refuses to accept America's mediocrity, lethargy or lack of concern when it comes to educating children.

There are three essential reasons why we need to teach students — and especially those who will one day be their teachers — explicitly about the reality of two Americas.

First, more than ever, stories of people who are different than the so-called "mainstream culture," namely people of color, immigrants or those whose lifestyle is labeled offensive because of dress or habit or sexual preference, have multiplied to the point of being a new majority. The United States has changed from below and the necessity of validating this reality grows with each year as new eyes and voices express what it means and feels like to be American. (Hasn't this always been the critical tension in America's society and literature?) The "Leave it to Beaver" years have been supplanted by single-parent households, individuals unafraid of their authentic selves, a highly mobile work force and sheer numbers of non-White Americans who could never have been accommodated in "the good old days." Without recognizing their experience in America — with minorities a majority in prison, the vast disparity in income differentials, a lack of health care access — we risk that a majority of students turn away from school as incapable of representing the most basic truths about their American experience.

The second and potentially more dangerous reason we must directly address America's dual nature, is that a nation in love with itself, its history and destiny is a very dangerous country. There were not a lot of nay-sayers or critics in Germany when The Third Reich came to power and reasserted Germany's rightful destiny. Nor did the Russian Revolution admit for decades that any part of its credo fell short of its lofty goals. Propagandists in China work well into the morning trying out official versions of "the truth." Raising children to believe that America has done no wrong and is permanently on the correct side of military disputes, economic development issues and international policy debates is prelude to disaster. In Greek theatre, it is always the tragic hero's own certainty of their rightness, and especially the justness of their cause which precipitates their descent into tragedy, as Creon learns so bluntly from Tireisias in *Antigone*:

> "These are no trifles! Think: all men make mistakes,
> But a good man yields when he knows his course
> is wrong,
> And repairs the evil. The only crime is pride."

And it is here that I must openly name the beast in the belly of the United States education establishment. Corporate media, the largest single shaper of mainstream information, are unwilling to fully acknowledge America's faults, shortcomings or historical devastations. Their inability to bridge the paradoxical gap which divides this country can be attributed to many things but principally because to do so would implicate themselves, negatively affect their bottom line and call into question the advantages and perquisites they take for granted. Most corporations would not stand for a full accounting of this country's historic, political and economic balance sheets, and they control the debate. They have even penetrated public policy to such an extent that the very rationale for mandatory public schooling, which has always been to create a skilled, knowledgeable and independent citizenry, has been subtly but conveniently shifted (starting with the 1984 report *A Nation at Risk*) toward simply providing our economy with acceptably skilled workers.

I strongly believe, as do many, that public school, under-girded by a foundation of free-inquiry and free-speech, supported by public monies and historically controlled at the local level, have a unique role to play in accurately, fairly representing the American experience. Their historic mission has been to build a strong base for democracy, encourage civic involvement, foster critical thinking and assist free inquiry so that there is actual wisdom behind the exhortation "a government of the people, by the people, for the people." Schools have never been and should not be today, as many suggest, simply about preparation for entry-level jobs, smoothing acceptance of the status quo or pumping up an uninformed patriotism in kids.

This is why the move toward uniform, standardized testing is so crucially important. The net effect of standardized exams is to foster an uncritical, unthinking approach to most of a student's learning and curriculum. It also determines what needs to be taught and for how long. Hidden underneath the correct answer for "Who was the first black person to play professional baseball?" lie the bones of thousands of Negro athletes, decades of official segregation and an historic racism which has resulted in tremendous barriers and unacknowledged effects on our society today. Yet, this question's primary function is to serve as a terminus for these larger issues. We are a better country for integrating blacks and minorities into many of our social structures, but we are not better off for ignoring, discounting or refusing to debate the attitudes and systemic prejudice which allowed for that kind of racism and criminality in the first place, as if it is all over now.

The third and final reason to accommodate and recognize two Americas within explicit education curriculum is, quite simply, because it is the truth: and recognizing truth is primary to freedom. We may consider ourselves a great nation because we have the world's biggest economy, strongest military, best science or most open society, but we will never be a truly great nation without developing what the world's wisdom traditions have always espoused as the most sublime quality: compassion. Compassion connotes a willingness to understand the suffering of another as if that pain were our own. It is, in fact, a kind of sacrifice for another, the basis of human love, relationship and community, and also, significantly, the fulcrum upon which education rests. With it true human freedom is possible; without it, nothing is: babies die, the sick go untreated, senior citizens are left to beggar in the streets. Acting on behalf of another — extending ourselves out of free will — is implicit in all that is great about America. Community barn raising has always been a more accurate depiction of immigrant life than the "pull-yourself-up-by-the-bootstraps" individualism imposed on our national consciousness.

America sees itself as a generous and kindhearted country, donating millions every year to house and feed the unfortunate. Our churches, mosques and temple halls regularly promote and sponsor social missions within their communities and beyond. Our *grande dame*, the Statue of Liberty, holds a torch of freedom and people come the globe over to steal a peak at her robes, view the blind justice which her scales represent. Is it really too much to ask that we take time in school to acknowledge those who have suffered or faced great hardship in coming to this land of freedom? Is it too burdensome to recognize and validate that many, perhaps a silent majority, never found their way free and went to defeat unlucky in liberty and self-determination? Doesn't our mixed history and heritage impel upon us, the survivors and the successful, even greater responsibility to work at improving our system?

Or should we allow someone to conclude, perhaps a person looking from afar, that the blindfold of Lady Liberty is more than symbolic — that we will, in fact, never face the challenging truth of our paradoxical identity?

Presenting the reality of two Americas means that accounts of misfortune, misdeeds and mistakes should be described, documented and discussed as often as stories about making it big. For every Rockefeller, mention of the millions of Depression hobos; with every discussion of macro-economic theory, a forum on homelessness; for every poster of a super-model or super-athlete, the face of an illegal alien ineligible for school or government aid. A truly "public" education should equip students to see the truth about who we really are and invite them to work toward a genuine love for that rather than provide false or incomplete images, then have them deteriorate into hypocrisy or cynicism as the years roll by. Truth has its own power to ennoble and energize. This conviction alone, that American society is willing to acknowledge that our great experiment is not yet complete or successful is exactly what is needed to ignite a fresh spirit of civic involvement and idealism in a new generation.

* * *

I imagine that there are a thousand Mrs. Whites out there today, putting on a brave face before the crowd, asking children to sing about the greatness of our country, even on cold mornings or when the object of their affection is less than deserving. What is simple and easy to believe is not always true; believing what is true is not always simple or easy. Or easy to capture in a song. We are a large, diverse, sprawling Republic; we "contain multitudes" as Walt Whitman said of himself.

It is now 50 years since *Brown vs The Board of Education* spelled out that "separate is not equal" when it comes to schooling children. And yet reality is, in the last decade, the tide of desegregation and equality has swung backwards and we now face concentrations of color and poverty similar to those in the early 1970s when my classmates and I first gathered around that flagpole. The sad thing is, we are not only not making progress: the front lines have been breached and whole communities are falling backwards onto themselves with little funding, support or national commitment to prevent it. The reality of two Americas is more dramatic and apparent than ever. All this under the banner of a policy entitled, *No Child Left Behind*, which holds that if students of color score as much as 15 percent less than white peers three years in a row, that school can be closed, the teachers fired and its administration taken over by the state.

I see now why I care so much about these things: we are simply heading in the wrong direction — blaming the wrong people — in trying to improve public education. And no one has encouraged me more in my effort to spell that out than my first teachers — my parents, confined to wheel-chairs in St. Cloud but having listened to these stories one-by-one over years, and wanting me to push for their publication even more than myself. Their strength and courage in facing the end of their lives makes me more determined than ever to fight for what I, and they, have always believed in — *freedom and justice for all*. Their idealism, the one that battled a depression, won a world war and piloted nine children through the baby-boom to college degrees, keeps me balanced, hopeful and focused on the dream that, one day, we will get it right.

As an educator, I am not required to believe America will cure its worst tendencies, that we will find ways to protect our environment, live peacefully with others or trade easy material gratification for something more substantial. Nor are my efforts contingent on enlightened education reform at the state or national level. I am not required to believe in anything except the importance of my students. They are what give me hope, the needed dose of optimism that propels me into action. What I get from them is intangible, immeasurable, wholly personal. Like leading a kind of family, looking out over a room of youngsters girds my determination that the next generation in America have it better than I did. Watching them grow and learn, I imagine that one day we will be able to see ourselves honestly, to realize that we are neither great, nor terrible, but an imperfect and idealistic people with an awesome responsibility to do what is right and fair, not just for ourselves anymore but for the world which we are considered to dominate.

There was nothing wrong with me, nor Horton, nor Fritz that early October morning in 1972; nor Mrs. White, nor Mr. Johnson, nor Vern the custodian who hung the flag up that morning before it was light. The problem was not even wholly the contradictory and hypocritical life of J. Edgar Hoover, as if any of us could ever be completely free of fault. The abiding problem that morning was that there was no possibility of admitting the complexity that adheres to the human character, which we sometimes study in school as history. That horrific things have been done under the rubric of very great principles, and that this may continue indefinitely; certainly, for as long as children are used to counterfeit a fraud about the greatness of things and people that are far more complicated than we realize.

post-script and mortems

Behind every book is the story of how it was written, where, when and at what cost in blood and treasure. Mine is no different, though, after a couple years of living dangerously — no salary, no health coverage, little human contact — the drama behind my curtain of words seems less remarkable, in need of new appurtenances. In Stephen King's *On Writing*, he talks about his two years as an English teacher in Maine and how hard it was to get any writing done, even on weekends; whereas, working blue-collar in a hot basement factory as he had in years previous, he wrote on breaks, at lunch and then late into the night at home. That's how he composed *Carrie*, the book that propelled him into a completely different universe, however steeped in school or besotted by horror. I identify, and do not particularly relish my return to being a limp after-school noodle and weekend slouch, constantly scanning units and paper loads while conducting odd inner debates about what to say in class. Yet, reality is, the time is nigh to do something reversely proportionate to what Mr. King did: leave my writing factory behind and get back to class.

We all have crosses to bear.

When I started writing this book, I had no notion of where it might lead. I wrote to discover. What I found was a lot of material from childhood, stories of family and early years in school. I see now that I did evolve a fairly complete outlook on teaching and that it had everything to do with my world growing up. That as much as I worked hard to become a good teacher, I never abandoned the primary importance of seeing the world through the eyes of that young learner. More recent experiences have felt less dramatic, less crucial to the elaboration of my message. And the odd truth is that part of my job all these years has been taking a giant eraser to my past, effacing my personal story so students could paint me in the way they needed, imagining a neutral but helpful adult in front of them. (Kids always do this: when you appear in line at the supermarket, they gush, "You mean you shop for food, Mr. Henry?") I also felt reluctant to use *their* stories as my own or those of *their* family's struggle or joy or uncertainty. Adolescence is but a portal, a small, important passage through which we pass on the way to what's beyond. I know how to help kids through but respect greatly their right to freedom and privacy once on the other side.

There is one thing though, which has surprised by magnifying and deepening over these years away: my absolute conviction that standardized testing, the imposition of state and federal authority over the content and progress of school curriculum is wrong, dangerous and must be stoutly resisted. And before I quit the public stage that is writing a book — or even get very far in this post-script — I need to say a few things about that. Namely, standards, as commonly conceived, are in fact the domestic equivalent of globalization: an attempt to obliterate any original or native customs and make them conform to a kind of bland uniformity which is ultimately hollow, degrading, and serves someone else's interest. If successful, they will reduce the thousand points of light in this country to a single dull bulb, vomiting facts and trivia and whose real effect is to render young people uncritically content with a lousy education, an unfair social contract and a deeply flawed national ethos which is hastening our planet's destruction.

As I write, Minnesota is on the forefront of this battle, a conservative governor and his mercenary education commissioner attempting to ram through an entire educational prescription for every child from kindergarten through 12th grade. (Hold your nose kid, stick out your tongue.) Along the way, standardized exams will inform the public as to who is making the grade, who is not. Presumably, rewards and punishment will follow. As number crunchers "disaggregate" test scores, the realization that minorities are faring poorly will put the focus on what we are doing wrong at school, while the rest of society turns its back on what is really undermining America: civic apathy, record income differentials, racial disparities, large scale corporatism run amok. Never mind that conservatives are successfully manipulating what gets taught and for how long, or that they regularly question the "patriotism" of those who object to their grand designs. The most important point is that they control the debate by using the rhetoric of "accountability": they compare schools against the business model and wave in taxpayers' faces, as matadors to a bull, the red cape of fear — fear of lower scores, fear of a declining economy, fear of there not being enough in the future — until the crowd calls out in chorus: "Blood! Blood! Blood!"

I recently saw a short news segment about standardized testing on CNN (a paragon of media excellence in comparison with competitors). "Yes," Minnesota's Education Commissioner sniveled, "there will be some loss of local control under the new system, but this is understandable because we live in such a highly mobile, integrated culture now and youngsters must be able to adapt and fit in as they move up the ladder or change schools or enroll in training. We need to know that every youngster has learned certain things." The reporter hemmed and hawed getting to the story's other side, his face serious, though neither his salary nor career were running much risk from his little curtsy at journalism. He finished in less than two minutes with this rejoinder: "Critics say that it will force teachers to teach to the test. But then, what's so wrong with that?" A long slow shudder ran down my spine.

Bar the door, Jocko!

The answer is, everything. To paraphrase William Butler Yeats, the Irish Poet and no small admirer of education: "Is education fundamentally about filling buckets or lighting fires?" Do we want to inspire young people to the magic of nature, science and the arts, or do we want them to sit like pails in a room while we douse them with facts, noting carefully who spits back the most? Children should, in fact, be *our teachers*. Buckminster Fuller believed that because they enter a (slightly) more evolved universe, they represent Nature's next tentative step toward an unknown goal it has pursued for millions of years — something more complex, more fully realized than we will ever understand. Children do inherit a tradition, yes; but they are also capable of seeing things in completely new and profound ways, of resolving entrenched problems and taking a passionate interest further than we ever imagined. Education's task is not to cheapen, control or subvert this, but to assist them, provide good harbor and encourage their contributions. Learning and the acquisition of knowledge is an instinct governed by forces greater than us; to co-opt that, make it routine or boring in service of merely commercial or political ends, is to destroy its integrity as a human endeavor.

What's wrong about teaching to the test is that life is not simply about deriving a "right" answer. What is the right answer to being alive? What is the right answer to a Rodin sculpture, a Da Vinci drawing or a Picasso painting? What is the right answer to the existence of the universe, the language of whales, the process of entropy? What is the right answer to creativity, the emotions of opera, the love we feel for each other? The correct answer is, more often than not, not a "right answer" at all. In fact, as science reveals, for every answer we generate, an infinity of new questions arise; and so, what we are really doing is constantly refining how much we do not know about nature, ourselves, the universe. And keeping ourselves afloat in such a sea of uncertainty, contingency, mystery means that learning is not about circling answers, but encouraging creativity, practicing collaboration, enhancing compassion, because these will have actual application in a world of unlimited answers.

179

The problem with teaching to the test is that one day a question will read this way:

1. *"Who was the greatest president of the 20th Century?*
    A.) Franklin Roosevelt   B.) John Kennedy
    C.) Theodore Roosevelt   D.) Ronald Reagan

The correct answer will be item D, and the student who misses will be under scrutiny, their search engines analyzed and diploma denied until they get it right. Standardization means that we want every child in America to derive the same conclusion from a given prompt, even when it papers over dubious assumptions and hidden judgments. Ones who get it wrong will be set aside, left behind and made less than others. The real goal of education should not be to have every child think the same, but to make certain every child *can think*, and *think critically*. To openly investigate for themselves who they consider the best president, conduct meaningful research, assemble a case using facts and logic, present it to peers orally or in writing and then listen to feedback and engage with them. We want students to create new learning, to analyze, synthesize, derive and create. In the real world we don't prize sameness but a quality of uniqueness: what we bring that no one else does.

Why teaching to the test injures is that it assumes learning is a zero sum game; that you either get it right or wrong in a competition in which only some succeed. Like with corporate capitalism, a few big winners take the best while the majority lose and must return to their shanty with fewer opportunities and less of a voice. It institutes a regime of fear and exclusivity which pits student against student, parent against parent, school against school, country against country. Scores must continually improve and grow, like the economy, even if as time goes on it becomes evident that by growing and improving we are destroying things and surrendering values we believe fundamental to happiness. Thus we pull the rug out from under our environment — extracting resources, spitting pollution, eliminating whole species of plants and animals — all because we have trained people to believe that what matters most in a zero sum game is that you resolve problems *as the system wants you to*. Your role is not to ask questions, but simply do as you are told: obey authority, observe your place. "Correct" behavior is the assurance you are not left in the cold, even though, because of unsustainability, we are guaranteeing the earth will one day go cold for everyone.

The dark shadow of teaching to the test is that success or failure in life will eventually come down to a number, and numbers are easily manipulated, changed, distorted. This can be done for an individual, a group or even across an entire district if enough people stand to benefit from the perception that scores have either gone up or down. Since the only thing that matters is the score — not skills, not an aptitude for human beings, not ethics or morals or integrity — cheating will grow as a means of getting ahead. Students will invent sophisticated ways to cheat using technology, while administrators will master the techniques available to them: dumbing the test, eliminating scores of certain groups, massaging statistics until they show only what the school district wants them to. Once this is permanently engrained in our culture — that appearances matter more than reality — we will begin producing generations with a cynical disregard for education, civil society and personal honesty.

The downside of teaching to the test is that right answers are often trivial and meaningless, that they are forgotten within weeks, that memory is in fact a low-order skill, that important information can be found more easily with computers, that what really makes businesses successful is a creative, innovative workforce not automatons, and that good teachers are quitting in droves because filling buckets is nothing beside the joy of lighting fires. Mostly the problem with teaching to the test is that it transposes the fear of the adult world — that we are slipping, that we can't compete, that the perverse Darwinian jungle we live in is a house of cards — onto the backs and psyches of children. Many are deeply terrified of scoring poorly, others could care less and circle answers randomly. Every child will be just as loveable, just as precious, just as important before the exam as after. The world will be just as complete and fulfilling if they score well as if they score poorly; and their fundamental needs — to be fed, to have loving relationships, to find creative outlets — will not change no matter what. The problem with teaching to the test is that it is absolutely inane, bears no relationship to what is important in life, consumes vast amounts of time and resources and informs everyone that learning *really is* boring, useless and to be avoided at all costs.

* * *

I can go on with the post-script now.

I may have given the wrong impression at the beginning about my experience writing this book. It hasn't really been about suffering at all. In fact, it's been one of the most precious periods of my life. Picture an ancient cabin of hewn logs on a small hill above a quiet river. Picture quaint out-buildings, well sunk, with strategic pines forming a kind of sheltered compound around a large tear-drop garden. Picture undulating hills beyond the yard, covered with grasses, flowers and trees and which slope gently toward the water. Picture a lone eagle heading home at dusk, flocks of ducks and geese whirring south in autumn, a matchless array of stars governing the night sky. Imagine the feel — doors gaping in the haymow — of winter sun, sharp tingles of open pores from rolling in snow after a sauna, the silky coat of an old Tom purring in your lap. Imagine waking at sunrise, reading a spell while nursing tea, having breakfast and then writing till mid-afternoon. Imagine a break, then dinner, then writing again until after midnight. Imagine that weekends, a beautiful woman appears with bags of groceries and news of the city. Imagine that this goes on for weeks, that seasons change, that whole wars are fought and won and lost and that a book gets written.

Imagine too, that there was another project during all of this: the building of a barn. Understand that it's as much a story as anything.

In 2001, our farmstead experienced its own bout of terrorism. An old barn burnt on a phenomenally windy day when local kids were off school. The fire left a whole in the yard, a kind of sadness in our lives as hobby farmers and kindled a determination that this would not stand. My wife and I made the decision to rebuild; thus, the fire also reduced to rubble savings I hoped would tide us through what might be termed my "writing thing."

Plans were assembled, debated, even argued over, a foundation was poured and walls framed in. Being that I had no ambition to ever construct another building in my life, I wanted to do something unique, notable, historically appropriate. I projected a basement — what is really the first floor here in Wisconsin — built of stone, seven feet tall running for almost 100 linear feet. I'll spare details for another day and just want to say that constructing it shed light on the inner debate I had been having about educational priorities. You might say I brought my other job with me to the work I was doing — cementing a wall, stone by stone.

You can't confuse me for a carpenter, but I know some that you can. What I lack in skill, attention to detail and the world of tools, they more than make up for. I noticed, when they were kind enough to allow me to work with them, that they live in a world where there is definitely a right answer. They are paid, and handsomely, to come up with right answers every day: to follow plans precisely, to make sure walls are plumb, level and square, that windows and doors fit snug.

Within limitations established by blue-prints however, there are myriad ways of arriving at the desired outcome. What tools are used, how to stage the work, which parts are assembled in what order, the quality of materials, how much tolerance for deviation is acceptable — all of these things can vary. For the answer — plumb, level and square — there are dozens of possible avenues. What seems to matter most in this is a kind of efficiency and common sense based upon experience, upon having framed walls a hundred times and knowing how the process should go. We hire carpenters based on their professionalism, on belief we have in their work and suitability for the project at hand.

I bring this up because I am intrigued by the insistence in educational settings on the consequence of right answers, on exactitude and precision when it comes to measuring what students are capable of. We want to know and understand precisely what it is they can and cannot do, whose skills and attributes shine and whose seem to be terminally in eclipse. We live in a world of exacting technology, where mistakes can have horrible consequences in human terms — I understand that and would not argue for a second that we can afford to go soft on nuclear engineering, medicine or even carpentry. But I would like to suggest that within the industry of school, we are insisting too soon and too much on the judgment of right and wrong, good and bad. Over the course of years and decades, what will matter most for kids becoming adults is their essential connectedness to the world they inhabit: relationships with people, a belief in community, a sense of their place in the natural order, and an excitement for what they want to do in life. Above everything else, these are the real priorities in schooling children.

Human beings are not as easily assembled as products or buildings, the logic of a plan and its execution subject to all kinds of contingencies, emotions, disputes, half-heartedness, gray areas, vulnerabilities and ambivalences. An inability by our educational institutions to adjust, refocus, adapt and recommit to the lives of young people — to where they are at — means we end up rejecting large numbers who have not necessarily signed up for the job of scholarship in math or science or literature and get turned off completely to the idea of education. That what makes for good carpenters and engineers and doctors is a passion for that kind of work, a person who applied themselves to learn everything they needed, undertook an educational process because they were caught by its possibilities and magic. Their eventual competence and professionalism gets built over time — and only by choice — is never fully resolved in a single instance of being right or wrong, but rather, is negotiated, developed and steadily progressed toward.

My friends the carpenters have framed up hundreds of walls; they do it extremely well, quick and efficient, and much better now than when they first started. They own their own business, tools, trucks and reputation for excellence, and make as much money as they want in a given year. They are especially adept at working with people, cajoling, assuaging, convincing, while nevertheless pinning them for a lot of money. Whatever promise they may have shown in high school, neither one ended up going to college and they don't seem any worse for wear.

Our culture, maybe more than any in history, insists on this level of professionalism and measured detachment in the way we go about work. We want professionals who are capable, calm and focused only on the job they have to do. To sing or dance or cry uncontrollably in the middle of performing a task would raise suspicions and fears about an individual's ability to set their humanity aside and do what we've asked them to. We don't necessarily want a personal relationship with our plumber or the meat inspector or the cable guy, or even to know much about them. Our system is set up to run without humanness gumming the gears, slowing progress or causing delays.

And so too, have we set about the business of schooling young people, trying to curtail as much as possible any shadings of subjectivity, value judgments or undue feeling. Far too often we clip wings early and insist that youngsters travel the shortest distance between two points without any flights of imagination. As mentioned earlier, schools are quite clearly reflective of larger social trends — in this case, bowing before the corporate ethos of control, efficiency, and suppression of individual difference. We are preparing them for an impersonal career and so we start them off right by making sure their education is not personal at all — that they, like everyone, must fit round pegs in round holes, square in square. The ones who can't seem to get that are sorted off and treated as if they have an original sin which can't be cured.

At times the job of teacher has made me feel like I am standing on the edge of this great abyss, polishing students and their skills before tossing them over the cliff into a world of products and professionalism, perhaps the last time anyone from the civil body of America will care so much about them. I recall vividly, deeply how this felt at that age: how crucial it was to get signals, confirmation, evidence that I was after all worthwhile, not only in an academic sense but as a human being, before heading out into the maelstrom. I had my share of tumbles, knocks, even rough edges, and that's what I've chosen to portray here; though over years, precious little of that has been of much tangible use with kids. What did work was frequent smiles, heartfelt thoughts about the material, a passion for play, some teasing, a tolerance for difference, a ton of acceptance and celebration, focused assessment of their writing, and at times, sadness over something hard happening quite close to us. My classes have always been very personal in this sense, and I have never hesitated to get close, ask after difficult issues and discover in kids the same basic goodness from which I am made. I learned as much as they and tried, whenever possible, to let them know that I care.

* * *

So, as well as writing a book, I built a foundation wall of stone and cement over the course of months. It was hard work, lifting stones, shoveling sand and cement, moving the form-work up and down, cleaning rock faces carefully after. I did it without carpenters or advice or even a lot of tools. Somehow working with stone and cement is closer to my sensibility than would be the precise cutting and fitting of carpentry. In a way, you could say that doing stonework is more personal. I like that it doesn't require electricity or a van full of tools. Also that there is a visible sense of improvement as I walk from the first side I worked on to the last. What I learned is observable in the finished product in a way I'm not sure would be true of carpentry. Finally, there is not a prescribed manner of building a stone wall. Yes, it must be within certain tolerances of height or width or uniformity, but except for the parameters of how the wall interacts with the wood, the rest is entirely flexible. In other words, it can be done in an infinite number of ways: which rock fits where, how the colors play, what corner stones get picked. There isn't a right answer. As a whole the barn looks great, but the truth is if it were done again tomorrow, because of my greater facility and the intuitive nature of the process itself, the rock wall portion would stack out completely different. Yet, paradoxically, as a matter of rough physics, it would appear much the same.

And so it must be said about this book. It has been written intuitively, reaching down for one stone at a time, looking for something that would fit, adding plenty of backing and aggregate, then packing it so that the whole thing would cure solid. I learned as I went, teacher and student, going without advice or professional help and spending considerable time cleaning up after. It came together as I imagined, though if I wrote it again tomorrow, because of my greater facility with words, it would be entirely different and as with my stone wall, in a way better; and yet paradoxically again, most likely, much the same. My values surrounding education would not change and nothing can redo the way I grew up; only the color and spacing and texture of how I reveal them. Thus we cement into words one particular version of our story and learn to accept it, warts and beauty all. As it hardens, there's no dodging responsibility for what's been done; it has to be okay.

Yet early returns from publishers are that it's not okay. The manuscript is "too personal," "too autobiographical," "too broad" even though it is nonetheless "very publishable," "intriguing," "compelling," "worthy," "timely," and other words intended to soothe. I can see how I did this wrong. Here I up and wrote a book, unspooled an entire narrative, without first seeking approval or obtaining a legitimate platform to speak to the public. I don't have the requisite connections to access a free press, or at least, there's no certainty I will obtain enough in sales to offset the risk that such a book might do a company material harm, not to mention potential embarrassment for supporting a teacher completely off-compass from most of America. If rejection is the badge a subversive must wear for firm principles, I will do so proudly and not retreat an inch of territory. I believe in naming the truth. But if it is merely that beneath the tent of media conglomeration only market trends are permitted to drive publishing decisions — and individual truth is judged solely on profitability — then I feel disheartened. With such a regime even best-sellers are not exquisite pearls as much as well-timed adumbrations of what the public wants to hear. That, to me, seems a recipe for literary and intellectual disaster.

Unlike public school, there is no one out here paid to listen or evaluate everyone's story. For that you need a therapist. And teachers, for the most part, are so damned blown-out at the end of the day, month and year that writing a book seems like a particularly bad idea much of the time. So it happens that we are not used to hearing from them. (As a publisher put it in a recent rejection: "Joe six-pack just doesn't care much about what happens at school or to teachers.") And anyway, learning that one once skipped school to throw a keg party, drop-started a bus with kids pushing or couldn't screw himself up to speak is exactly what the public wants to block out, caught as we are in our own fancy of professionalism: an image of a full human being teaching children a little too naked to handle. Too personal.

And yet, the rest of the world, for my taste, seems a bit too impersonal. Those carpenters of mine, who worked on the barn, one of them grows his own food, cans vegetables, makes home-made wine and likes to noodle on the guitar; the other speaks with a noticeable German accent, is fussy about his teeth, has a black standard poodle and enjoys traveling. He's serious, well-spoken and sports a short hair style; the other is laid back, bearded and looks like the hippie Jesus. Together they're an unbeatable team. They're actually friends of mine, and unlike more standard carpenters, their small eccentricities are precisely what I treasure about them. It's also roughly the same thing I like about my barn's stone wall — in all its imperfection — and why I don't regret writing this book without first seeking a go ahead or even questioning if it was a good idea.

In fact, the willingness to take a non-standard approach may be my greatest asset in working with students. Kids especially enjoy spontaneity, originality, the feeling they are going someplace new with an appointed guide. There is something irreducible and entirely American about going after life with the zest and originality of a hopeful amateur — unafraid, and at times, unaware of the possibility of mistakes. That may be the founding principle of our country: our constitution having been assembled by principled dabblers in affairs of state who learned as they went, not to mention the legions of improvisational immigrants who followed in their wake.

I insist again here at the end: We are all students; we are all teachers. The best among us head out confident, learning as much as we can and end up teaching to others the better part of what we learn. In my case, in becoming Mr. Henry, that what is unique and imperfect about us creates our humanity: our quirks and quakes and quickenings the precise ingredients which make us loveable. May they be the last things washed out, no matter how professional a world we fall into. And let's hope they are always the first things we look for and celebrate about children.